"Timothy Gaines understands that knowing God means far more ~~~~~ ~~~~~ ~ about God. In *Walking the Theological Life*, Gaines introduces students to theology through the lives of biblical figures, each transformed by the living God amid the nitty gritty of their daily lives. With the gift of a good storyteller and the wisdom of a seasoned professor, Gaines casts a vision for the kinds of people we're invited to become in order to know and love God, even if we never join the theological academy. I thoroughly enjoyed reading this book and can't wait to get it into the hands of my students."

Emily Hunter McGowin, associate professor of theology at Wheaton College and author of *Christmas* in the Fullness of Time Series

"I wish to extend my sincere appreciation to Timothy Gaines, who authored such an excellent work. Furthermore, I sincerely congratulate the theological and academic circles in the United States for producing a young theologian who demonstrates the essence of theological life with such a comprehensive and balanced perspective. If I had read this book thirty years ago when I began my theological studies, I have no doubt that I would be a better theologian. The book presents a remarkable and persuasive discourse on what it means to live a theological life through profound biblical interpretation and theological understanding, avoiding fossilized theological methodologies."

Hwarang Moon, professor of worship at Korea Theological Seminary

"By examining the stories of people in Scripture who are just as flawed as we are, Timothy Gaines moves us beyond simply memorizing precepts of theology and instead provides compelling evidence that theology may be best understood as we examine who God is in relation to his people. I highly recommend this book for anyone who wants to move beyond the need for absolute certitude in one's faith, and instead is willing to swim about in the mystery of a God who exceeds anything we can imagine."

James K. Hampton, professor at Asbury Theological Seminary

"This book is an extraordinary invitation to engage (and perhaps wrestle!) with thinking theologically in deeply formative ways. Timothy Gaines proves to be an excellent guide, bringing into conversation important biblical figures, key theologians (such as Augustine, Barth, and Jennings), and his own reflections. This bridge of theological method and virtue formation takes seriously the task of spiritual formation for the reader, demonstrating how thinking theologically through story continues to be transformative, complex, embodied, and dynamic. Engaging and beautifully accessible, this work is a gift for both the academy and the church."

Jennifer Matheny, George W. Truett Theological Seminary at Baylor University

"*Walking the Theological Life* reminds us of the joy of theology done rightly. Drawing on the stories of several (often quite imperfect) biblical characters facing various situations, we hear the message that theology is foundational for each of us, even those of us who are quite imperfect. The theme throughout is formation—the goal of theology is not simply to shape our thoughts but to draw us toward the virtues necessary for the life of faith."

Steve Wilkens, professor of philosophy and ethics at Azusa Pacific University

"More than telling people about theology, volumes of which abound, Gaines invites us into thinking about theology in new, enlivening, and constructive ways. He is inviting people to reconceive the theological task in ways that the Bible itself exemplifies: in real lives, in formative and engaging ways. This is a primer on how the theological work can continue in coming generations and, as so, a book I'm eager to share with undergraduates and seminarians alike who seek to know and reflect God but have felt alienated from the academic contexts."

Patrick Oden, research associate professor of theology at Fuller Theological Seminary

WALKING *the* THEOLOGICAL *Life*

DISCOVERING METHOD FOR THEOLOGY IN THE LIVES OF BIBLICAL CHARACTERS

TIMOTHY R. GAINES

Academic

An imprint of InterVarsity Press
Downers Grove, Illinois

InterVarsity Press
P.O. Box 1400 | Downers Grove, IL 60515-1426
ivpress.com | email@ivpress.com

InterVarsity Press® is the publishing division of InterVarsity Christian Fellowship/USA®. For more information, visit
intervarsity.org.

The publisher cannot verify the accuracy or functionality of website URLs used in this book beyond the date
of publication.

Cover design: David Fassett
Interior design: Daniel van Loon
Cover Image Credits: Getty Images © mikroman6 / Moment, © AdrianHillman / iStock, Images from The Holy Bible,
           containing the Old and New Testaments. Oxford: University Press; London: sold by E. Gardner,
           1853. Pdf. https://www.loc.gov/item/78317681/.

ISBN 978-1-5140-0743-3 (print) | ISBN 978-1-5140-0744-0 (digital)

Printed in the United States of America ∞

Library of Congress Cataloging-in-Publication Data
A catalog record for this book is available from the Library of Congress.

31   30   29   28   27   26   25   24 | 13   12   11   10   9   8   7   6   5   4   3   2   1

For Shawna

Contents

Acknowledgments

OFFERING A BOOK TO READERS is nothing short of participating in an economy of gift. As this book was coming into being, there were images in my mind of offering it as a gift to those who are wading into theological waters, whether for the first time or as those who still do not know whether theology is for them. I could imagine readers approaching the shore the way we do when we are not sure whether we really want to get wet: the first plunge can be uncomfortable, shocking, exhilarating, or thrilling, usually all at the same time. I would imagine this collection of reflections as something like an inflatable lounge chair that holds you in the water, looks a bit inviting from the dry land, and maybe even helps you want to be in the water more—a gift offered to those to invite them in.

Offering a gift like that, however, depends on a series of gifts that have been given to me. My students have given me gifts of encouraging feedback as these reflections took shape in lecture form. For all they knew, they were simply reacting in real time to their notions of theology being reshaped by an encounter with biblical narratives. To me, their wide-eyed reception of this content was a gift of affirmation that the approach in these pages might be useful to others as well.

A collection of writer colleagues huddled in the warmth of a retreat center amid a snowy Chicago winter lavished gift upon gift in the form of insightful editorial commentary and suggestions for exploration, but most of all friendship along the journey of writing. Thank you to Tara

Edelschick, Michael Jordan, Emily McGowin, and Kathy Tuan-Maclean for journeying together as our respective writing projects were taking shape; you all were and are a means of grace. Thanks also to Michaele LaVigne for bringing the compelling wisdom and keen insight of a spiritual director to bear on the project. Her investment of time has undoubtedly opened a pathway of growth. My gratitude abounds for Lori Neff, Al Hsu, David McNutt, Rachel Hastings, and the rest of the team at IVP who have spoken creatively into this effort.

Thanks also to the various congregations, including my own, that have allowed me to work some of this content out in homiletical form. I have cherished the conversations at churches and retreats that flowed from learning from the lives of these biblical figures. My friend Zack Church gifted me one of the jokes contained in the chapter on Sarah. I will not reveal which one in case you do not find it as funny as I did.

The true gift of a sabbatical to write this book came from my friends and colleagues at Trevecca, for whom I am constantly grateful. Thanks especially to Shawna, Callen, and Evalynne, who have exhibited understanding, patience, and grace. Your life and love are true demonstrations of the economy of gift, gifts I receive with gratitude beyond description.

INTRODUCTION

Invitation to Theology

LATELY I HAVE LOOKED INTO BRIGHT EYES, newly opened to the wonder of theology. To look into these eyes is at once thrilling and frightening. The thrill emerges first. It takes deep, hidden root and then quickly crackles to the surface of my skin, where a chill brings the hair on my arms to attention. I often get chills when a student makes a connection for the first time or offers an insight that enriches the theology we are doing. The fear is close behind. I am terrified at the prospect of leading astray students, through some lack on my part, who have entrusted themselves to my teaching. But more than that, I fear that my own limitations will somehow stunt the invitation to walk the theological life, reducing an awe-inspiring summons to nothing more than a set of information and concepts to be mastered for the sake of making a grade. I fear that the thrill of theology will be rendered uninspiring, and I will be to blame.

When I stumbled into it, theology became a gift I could not have dreamed up on my best day. For one who had been fascinated by the things of God since childhood, finding theology was like the beginning of an adventure into the far country, launching out from the safe and nurturing harbors of home for the quest of a lifetime. Laid open before me was a field of exploration into the deepest questions of human life, a horizon on which longing spirituality and the world's most pressing issues met, a subtle invitation for my wandering and ambitious heart to find a home in God. Churning in the deepest places of my motivation was the desire to know the goodness and love that was making the world new and to facilitate others in coming to know it as well. For me, theology became a lifeline to connect my calling to a two-thousand-year-old, worldwide community of people who understood that kind of longing. Often, opening a theology book connected me to a friend in its author, someone who shared a similar longing who could somehow reach out through the pages, put an arm around me, and invite me to take the next steps on the journey. Quite simply, theology was adventurous, joyful work.

Eventually, I found that not everyone took to theology like this. Persisting like weeds propagating from thousand-year-old seeds, some approaches to theology have grown into attempts to calcify answers about the divine, to take them neatly in hand, and to bring an unwieldy world under our theological control. These are the approaches, I fear, that, like weeds, choke the wonder out of love. I am all for good theology, of course, and especially the kind that draws us into the blindingly brilliant truth of the divine. So too am I glad for the vital, careful, and measured work of theology, assessing the faithfulness of a particular concept or statement the way a parent might examine the trustworthiness of a cradle that will hold their infant. Yet, theology as I have come to know it does more than maintain the right ideas in mind or provide the necessary skills to become a certified doctrine inspector. As helpful as these aspects of theology are, they are not its whole, and those who accept an invitation to do theology like this alone will condemn themselves to live in several small rooms of an expansive dwelling. We can come to theology expecting it to give us a few answers about God, or some moral positions to hold on to, and if this is our approach, theology will deliver. But we can also come to theology as one summoned to a world of wonder, joy, and astounding discovery. The way you approach theology will shape the kind of theologian you become, which will inevitably form the kind of theology you produce. And so here at the outset, I ask you, "What does an invitation to theology look like to you? Where do you think this will take you? To what do you think you are being invited? Who do you hope to become as you accept this invitation?"

Throughout my years as a theology professor and pastor, it has become evident that not everyone has this same receptivity to theology's invitation. This is where my fear returns: Will the invitation I offer to study theology act as an expansive gateway to the adventure of a lifetime, or will it be a passageway into a cramped, locked room? Across the years, I have heard the complaints of those for whom theology seems intimidating, difficult, or of little use. It probably does not help that most people in this position are beginning a theology course with a section on method. Straightforwardly, theological method is the examination of *how* theology is done. It is good, necessary reflection because the way we do theology shapes the results. Explorers, for example, will make different kinds of discoveries if they take a waterway route rather than an overland passage. Some routes we take can lead to thrilling discovery, others to disaster. It is important to pay attention to *how* we go about our work.

For many, though, beginning with method dulls the wonder of the invitation. It can feel like the mandatory safety briefing before we get to the journey. It is necessary, yes, but can be a bit disconnected from the adventure. Maybe, then, the discontent with theology is not a problem with theology itself. Maybe it is a problem with the invitation.

This is why I would like to offer an invitation to theology that does not lose theology's sense of wonder. It is entirely possible to examine theological method in a way that not only inspires but also calls us to a full-bodied entrance into the theological life, in which the way we do theology is just as much about who we are becoming as it is about how we construct concepts. My desire for this approach does not grow out of some scheme to simply grow theology's market appeal but is rooted in and nourished by the way humans across history have been inspired to theology's journey. Throughout most of Christian history, the invitation to theology has come not as a discipline disconnected from who we are but as an offer to respond to God from the deepest parts of who we are. Unquestionably, giving attention to method—the *way* theology is done—is important, though oftentimes the deepest joy of doing theology is when the *how* is deeply connected to the *who*. As vital as methodology is, theology is often introduced by wading through the conceptual maze that is contemporary theological method, too often leaving imagination unsparked and virtue undeveloped among those first meeting the discipline.

That is why this book will serve as an invitation to the adventurous joys of the theological life by first developing the virtues necessary for the work of theology. It will introduce readers to various methodologies and methodological issues, though it will not serve to catalog each methodology, as many other fine contributions have done. Our exploration of theological method comes by way of giving attention to the virtues the Christian community across the ages has held up, and asking how those virtues might shape who we are and how we approach theology. Those called to the vocation of theology have an astounding and thrilling privilege of responding to God, proclaiming in provocative and nuanced ways the astonishing reality that God is redeeming a beloved creation in beautifully surprising ways. The kind of response we offer, though, will undoubtedly be shaped by *who* we are. Many people can receive news; the character of those persons will shape how they respond to it.

FORMATIONAL VIRTUE

I am drawing here on what Nicholas Wolterstorff calls *formational theology*, the kind equipped to "mine the tradition . . . to see what we can learn about cultivating the Christian virtues."[1] In a formational approach, we seek to develop the virtues of the one called to the work of theology, not only so that the joys of theology might be awakened in us but also so that we are formed well to engage in the work of studying history, doctrine, and Scripture. In short, I want to take up these sacred stories with attention to how knowing is far more than possessing information; it goes to the level of formation, even sanctification.

A formational invitation to theology also has the capacity to heal the methodological rupture between doctrine and practice, overcoming the

---

[1]Nicholas Wolterstorff, "To Theologians: From One Who Cares About Theology but Is Not One of You," *Theological Education* 40, no. 2 (2005): 90.

divide between what Wolterstorff calls engaged theology—a theology of and for the church—and nonengaged theology, which proceeds theoretically. When the invitation to theology is posed as an invitation to nonengaged, theoretical forms of theology, it is a particular challenge to those who come to theology suspicious of its worth for the work of the church. What I offer here, then, is a formational theology approach to theology broadly. It is an attempt to recast the invitation to theology by going back to one of its original invitational forms: the stories of Scripture.

SCRIPTURE AND VIRTUE

Though Scripture offers far more than accounts of virtue, the stories of some of our ancestors in the faith offer a summons to do the work of theology virtuously. The biblical figures we will examine are not proto-theologians who unlock the technical secrets of how theology should proceed in the twenty-first century. They are not all even particularly virtuous figures, at least in a conventional sense. These are simply people who responded to God. Their stories, though, offer images that the Christian community across the ages has upheld as virtuous responses to God's activity. While these stories can be the seedbed for doctrinal work, we are going to ask what they have to teach us about method—*how* we do the work of theology virtuously, precisely because of *who* these people are in their responses to the divine. In other words, I want to read them invitationally; the virtues we find in them for *how* to do theology also become an open door to doing theology itself. In them, we have methodological gestures that are also alluring, invigorating encouragement to take up the joys of theology. These stories are images of what I am referring to as the *theological life*, a term I am using in a broad sense to encompass the lives of those called to theology in its many forms: academic, professional, pastoral, general interest, and so on. The theological life is where the work of theology and theological virtue meet, expressed twelvefold in the chapters to follow.

Overall, though, linking theological method to virtue allows for a fresh, enlivening wind to blow through the beginning points of theology.

Where once theological method was largely a series of intellectual commitments guiding a larger project, it can, through the lives of these biblical figures, now account for courage, laughter, doubt, grief, and the like. In turn, their stories are an invitation for courageous, laughing, doubting, grieving people to the wondrously joyful work of theology. These are stories, stirred up under the influence of the Spirit's inspiration and later preserved as sacred Scripture precisely because they signal to the communities that grant them authority that there are certain virtues that have allowed people to respond and know God well. Thomas's doubt, for example, is not a simple morality tale; it is a demonstration of how doubt might be stewarded virtuously on our way to proclaiming, "My Lord and my God!" Laughter, as we see in Sarah's life, may not be incidental to her story; it can also be a signal to her progeny of how one might respond well to God's surprising work.

Undoubtedly, we could turn to many others, but I have selected these twelve not only for what I find in their lives but how my life as a theologian is found in them. I can see my insecurity in Jeremiah. Like Martha, I have known grief. I resonate with Thomas's doubt. I need Miriam's courage. With Jacob, I wrestle. Taken together, this is a company of often unsaintly saints who issue permission to reply to God with a full-bodied response. Cracked vessels though they may be, their lives pour forth a narrative stream of how humans have encountered God across the ages and how those encounters have evoked a response. Theirs is no one-size-fits-all response to God, but among the varied responses, we can find virtues that constitute the theological life. In their stories, we find reactions to God that know nothing of separating who they are as persons from their response to God. These are perfectly imperfect people who rarely struggled with applying theology to life because they never assumed that theology could be separated from life. Their encounters with the divine happen in the midst of real-life situations, and their example will teach us, for better or worse, that our response to the divine happens in real life, in the midst of real situations, and that sets the table for doing theology in joyful love and service.

John Webster has it right when he claims, "Being a Christian theologian involves the struggle to become a certain kind of person, one shaped by the culture of Christian faith."[2] The stories of Scripture are culture-creating narratives, not only giving us a story that makes sense of who we are as theologians but also establishing the virtues of the theological life. This is also why I offer a prayer at the conclusion of each chapter. Theology is a life of prayer, and one delightful aspect of the figures we will examine is that in their witness, you cannot quite distinguish theology from prayer. That is a distinctive feature of the theological life and a virtue for the work of theology that traditional methodologies alone struggle to instill. A lot of people can study theology. Walking the theological life is a different kind of thing.

This strikes me as good news for those who may be approaching the work of theology with fear, suspicion, indifference, or some mix of all of these. "I just don't want to get things wrong about faith or God," I will often hear. "This probably isn't going to apply to my life or ministry, but I need to make sure I get it straightened out." "I'm not sure what theology is," others will courageously admit, "but I know I'm afraid of it." Valid as these sentiments are, my hope is that an invitation to the theological life through the figures you are about to encounter not only gives these sentiments a place but also helps us to orient these fears and frustrations toward virtuous theological work.

Taking the time to develop the virtues of the theological life is an act of love for God and for those we serve, including those we have not met yet. Whether you are doing theology for pastoral, academic, or some other purpose, there will probably be a time when a child in your care asks a question about God at bedtime. You may find yourself helping a community grapple with painful loss or widespread injustice. A family member may call you to offer a devotional thought or prayer at an event they are celebrating. Perhaps a person in your church who has just been thrust unwillingly into the throes of grief will look at you and ask where

---

[2]John Webster, *The Culture of Theology*, ed. Ivor J. Davidson and Alden C. McCray (Grand Rapids, MI: Baker Academic, 2019), 45.

God is in their pain. In those moments, it can be an abundant gift to have, years before, joined Miriam in her courage, to have learned from Jacob's wrestling, Mary's pondering, or John the Baptist's edgy prophetic witness. You may not have precise words, but you will have a character nurtured by their theological virtue. Developing these virtues in the company of the saints will create in us the freedom to do the work of theology as grief, courage, and prophetic proclamation, employing holy reason "in exemplary submission to the gospel."[3]

This, then, is your invitation to theology. It is a summons to the adventure of responding to God by developing the characteristics of those who have come before us and who pass on to us the profoundly good news of the gospel. The theological life stands open to you, not because you have mastered every point of doctrine or taken in every fact of Christian history but because God is catching you up in the divine work of making all things new through the way of a crucified and resurrected carpenter. Describing and proclaiming that work will call for us to be certain kinds of people, steeped in the virtues of speaking and embodying the gospel. Gladly, we have exemplars in that work who have come before us, and to their lives we now turn.

---

[3]John Webster, *Holiness* (Grand Rapids, MI: Eerdmans, 2003), 27.

CHAPTER ONE

Jeremiah

ON NOT KNOWING HOW TO SPEAK

THE WORD OF GOD CAME TO a young man, living somewhere among the flatlands north of Jerusalem: "Before I formed you in the womb I knew you" (Jer 1:5). It is an odd way to begin a prophetic epic. There are no specific commands, no calls to action. Rather, it is this: "I know you. I have always known you." It is a God-breathed message in the form of an anticipatory pause. Jeremiah is about to be called to speak profound and challenging news.

When we find him, Jeremiah is poised to be launched into an active prophetic life: proclaiming a burning message he cannot hold inside, calling his people to reverse course on their path to destruction, being thrust into the middle of controversy and intrigue when confronting false prophets, and passionately weeping over a people he loved. On top of that, he is young and untested. The wisdom of years has not yet been formed in him. If there is anything he knows with certainty, it is that he is utterly unqualified to speak for God. Humility undoubtedly characterizes him, and not the type that has been cultivated in his character over decades. No, this is the kind of humility that bursts out of the raw reality that Jeremiah has no training or experience in calling a people to turn away from destruction or confronting those who fancy themselves religious leaders. He is young, underqualified, and untested—a good friend to any of us who take the first halting and uneven steps toward walking the theological life, knowing deep in our bones that we simply are not prepared for any of this.

Before the prophetic confrontations begin, however, there is a cherished moment of silence, where a simple, profound reminder establishes everything that will transpire: God *knows* Jeremiah. Oh, I am sure God knows *about* Jeremiah, too, in the sense of knowing what he likes to eat and the color of his eyes, but that is not what God is trying to relay to this young prophet-to-be. The divine voice speaks of intimate, deep, personal knowledge, the kind that has the capacity to see beyond the color of Jeremiah's eyes into the depths of his motivations, fears, and desires. This is the kind of knowledge reserved for parents and the children who make their every need known, spousal lovers of fifty years, childhood friends who now share stories about their grandchildren, and the God who lovingly breathed life into the lungs of each person who has been created. Jeremiah, a young man who is about to take on an active and harried ministry of preaching and proclamation in the midst of a messy and complex world is, quietly, deeply, and truly, known by God.

KNOWN TO KNOW

From the beginning, I cannot resist doing a little theology here. What kind of a God is this who would begin a conversation not with a command but with a reminder of the relationship? *Before* I formed you in the womb, I knew you. We could easily move into all kinds of theological speculation about things like divine foreknowledge and predestination at this point. We could spend a long time debating the theological merits of describing a God who could somehow know a not-yet-existent Jeremiah and who had charted a path before the young man had emerged from the womb. But the text does not ask us to go there, and if we did I fear we would be stretching it further than it asks us to. It does seem to say, however, something about the way God confronts with a call to speak a divine message. Jeremiah's response can teach us about the theological virtue of being known by God. We could say that Jeremiah exhibits a general virtue of humility, because he proceeds not by reaching out for knowledge but by acknowledging that he is known by God. But Jeremiah exhibits a more specific *theological* virtue because he is known by *God*, and Jeremiah's knowledge will humbly progress from that point. Even his knowledge is a response to God's intimate act of knowing Jeremiah. From the beginning, this is a God who *knows* us.

Knowing like this, though, situates the theologian oddly in our world that seeks to know. We live and move and have our being in a world of -ologies, those branches of scientific exploration that have as their mission to know more about the things they study. Is theology any different? At first glance, it may seem the most natural thing in the world for a theologian to study God the way a biologist studies a plant, because of the way we have come to think about *knowing* in the modern world.

The world you and I inhabit is the kind that has been built on the structures of the Enlightenment. Granted, some approaches to theology are happy to adopt these structures and continue to build the project, and others are reacting against it, but whether for it or against it, the Enlightenment looms large. While I am admittedly reaching for a broad brush in the depiction of the Enlightenment I am about to offer, there is an enduring theme—even a type of modern virtue—to the Enlightenment's ways of *knowing*.

The Enlightenment was itself a reaction against the perception that the ways of knowing that characterized the Middle Ages were lodged in superstition and claims about the truth of things that were not accessible to all people. But what if there was some kind of truth that all people could access? Or better yet, what if we could finally verify that there was one, single, objective truth that holds all things together under our watchful gaze? What if we were able to move beyond the enchanted and fantastic tales of some people sensing a divine presence while others were left unaffected? After all, what good is a truth if only a few people have access to it?

The proponents of Enlightenment thought came to affirm that we humans could begin to use our senses to verify the way things are in the world. In other words, we could *know* through our powers of observation.

And power is precisely what observation afforded us. Once we had enough people who could observe the same thing, a confidence began to grow in the Enlightenment mind that at long last, we were gaining access to verified, cold, hard truth, free from the whims of subjectivity and superstition. Ways of knowing—such as the scientific method—came to be associated with *objectivity*, and with objectivity came the notion that we could finally eliminate the persistent and mysterious unknowns about our world. Objectivity, unaffected by personal desire or whim, was now a virtue of modernity.

Imagine a person attempting to know something about the way a bird flies. When our eye beholds a winged creature, gracefully held aloft by some invisible force, there is more than a bit of mystery involved. As we make reasoned observations, however, we might finally come to observe that the way a bird flies on a windy day may differ from a day when the winds are calm. We might look at the shape of a bird's wing and observe how similar shapes act in the air. Step by observable step, we strip away the mysteries of a bird's flight to *know* how they are able to take to the skies. At the same time, we can finally put to rest the pesky debate our pre-Enlightenment ancestors might have had about whether birds are kept in flight by, say, a magical force they each possess in their bellies, or whether an invisible angel carries each bird from place to place.

There are obviously a multitude of benefits that have come about as a result of this kind of knowing. Knowing how birds fly inspired the innovations that allowed humans to take to the skies, for example. Nearly every scientific discovery made in the past few centuries sought to know by stripping away the shroud of mystery so that we might make use of newfound knowledge. Once we understand the physical forces of pressure that form above and below a bird's wing, for example, we *have* that knowledge, and now we can do something with it. The mystery of flight was finally pressed into giving up its secrets to the inquiring mind that came to know it. In this dynamic, the modern mind tends to take possession of a thing by knowing it, to assert the knower over the thing known. When we have erased the mystery, we have become the master.

So, the Enlightenment project continues to be built, often by those who gain knowledge through studies—even earning *master*'s degrees along the way.

What if theologians approach knowledge differently, though? Put another way, what if theology's methods do not share the same goal as those of our colleagues in physics, biology, chemistry, or the social sciences? What if the theologian maintained a distinctive approach that did not seek to strip away mystery for the sake of mastery but to plunge headlong into the mystery—not in hopes of stripping the mystery away so that we might master it but by surrendering into it, deferring, being known by it? What if we approached the work of theology by acknowledging the reality that the God we want to know is the one who knows us first? How might adjusting our way of knowing from first being a knower to being known shape the kind of theology we do? Theology has the capacity to celebrate scientific discovery, learn from our partners in the social sciences, and foster deep appreciation and conversation from those in other fields, even as it recognizes that the nature of our quest is not to take knowledge in hand, for the one we seek to know has known us first.

Young Jeremiah's prophetic proclamations issue a cautionary and liberating word to those of us who unwittingly attempt to know God inside of the Enlightenment's project. This is not only because any knowledge we master will, by definition, be limited and thus incomplete, but because such ways of knowing distance us from the stunning beauty that is theology's own: God knows us. For those who seek to unravel the mysteries of the divine for the sake of finally grasping it in hand, Jeremiah's liberating message also comes to us: before you go about the task of attempting to know God, know that you are first known by God.

The opening lines of Jeremiah's prophecy are a birthing suite for the virtuous work of knowing and being known in the task of theology. What is born out of his words is not an attempt to know for the sake of mastering but an invitation to first be known by God. As Jeremiah has it, the beauty of God is no set of hidden facts that, once unveiled through inquiry and observation, can be held in our hands as we would possess an idol of wood or bronze. We are known, rather, by a *living* God. We might be able to know the equations that describe how lift, drag, thrust, and weight function in lifting a bird aloft, but we cannot be *known by* those forces. Before we speak about God, before we put pen to paper or utter a single word, there is this: we are known by God. We could say it another way: before theologians set out to know God, they are known by God.

On its face, a claim such as this may come off as if we are casting being known by God in a spiritual light, while knowing God remains in the dusty and dull domain of theology. Jeremiah did not see these as opposing realities, though, and we would do well to follow Jeremiah's lead here, because the implications for the way we do theology are revolutionary. The weight of knowing shifts from whatever kind of knowledge we can derive about the divine to being known by God. We are known by God before we have the capacity to know anything about God. Contingent and wispy are all our attempts at knowing. God has known us first, even before we could know back. Rather than serving as a way of ordering the world under our mastered knowledge, our knowing orders us as creatures lovingly known by God.

The beginning of the theologian's quest to know God is in being known by God, placing all of us in a posture of epistemic humility and prayerful wonder. For the theologian, this posture even gestures to the beginning of a method. We begin by acknowledging that God knows us. We sit with that, we wonder at that, and it begins to suggest to us a way of doing our work. We are searched and known, to borrow the language of the psalmist (Ps 139:1). Our motivations, our gifts, our biases, our fears, our anxieties, hidden and unveiled, bravely acknowledged or naively undetected—all of that is taken up in the way God encounters us, *knowing* us. How might this shape the kind of theology we do? How might this move theology from the quest to acquire information about God for the sake of having answers and reorient it toward a kind of awareness that we are known by God first and beginning from there?

For the theologian, all of who we are is brought to the work of theology. A biologist may be able to check their personhood at the door, and the physicist may even be encouraged to do so. *Who* they are should not shape the results of their work, we are told. They are to be objective observers for the sake of unveiling knowledge. But theologians assume a different kind of posture. The beginning of our work is to be known by God, to open ourselves to the mystery that God has known *us*. Before we speak, we are known by God.

KNOWING AND SPEAKING

Perhaps there was wisdom in young Jeremiah's response, then. "Ah, Lord GOD! Truly I do not know how to speak" (Jer 1:6 NRSV). In hope that you will afford me a moment of personal catharsis: I have been doing the work of theology in the church, university, and seminary for most of my life, and oh, what I would give for theologians who were aware that they did not know how to speak. In all of those arenas, there is an impulse, a driving temptation, even, to speak as if we know—and know rightly!—before we are content to be known. Could it be that the one who is least aware of the reality that they are known by God is the one who most often wishes to speak first? The wisdom of Jeremiah, I think, is here: When you become aware that you are known by God, it is not wrong to confess, "I don't know how to speak." In his response, we detect no hint of bloviating self-confidence, no agenda-driven argument, no epistemic arrogance that somehow Jeremiah will be able to craft any words worth uttering. The word of the Lord has come to him. It has made him aware that he is known by God, and he is beautifully aware that he has nothing to say in response.

Straightforwardly, the word of God comes to young Jeremiah, and his response is simply, "I don't know how to speak!" In my estimation, the most faithful theology begins here, in the encounter between a God who has known us, who has called us, and our confession that we really do not have anything to say in response. Jeremiah's first words are his confession that he has no words. Yes, the words will come. How could one remain silent in the sustaining knowledge that one is known by the living God? But for now, and right here at the beginning, Jeremiah's theological work is his brave confession: "I don't have anything of my own to say. I have no words." There is something of virtue here.

"I AM ONLY . . ."

Jeremiah's accompanying confession, "I am only a boy!" carries a certain kind of cultural baggage (Jer 1:6 NRSV). In his tribe, at that time, humans became more important with age. Gray hair was a crown of glory; wisdom came with years. It is what Jeremiah lacked that fascinates me most. "I am only . . ." has me thinking about the way that theology is so often treated in places such as universities and seminaries. We construct grand buildings and invite those who hold grand titles to help us talk about God, and for many of us this is the beginning point of theology. For many of us, our confession of "I am only . . ." describes a lack of capacity, an absence. For Jeremiah (and I can only hope for the work of theology), it is a mark of theological virtue. It is a signal to the reality that he presents no credibility based on his mission of discovery, nor exhibits his self-made capacity to speak for God. "I am only . . ." This is the first step in walking the theological life virtuously.

For all of us who come to the task of theology with Jeremiah's words on our lips, or at least that kind of humility in our hearts, I say, "Well done." To those who begin a theological journey with a sense of trepidation and uncertainty, I say, "You are in the right place." To those who come to the task of theology full of confidence, I offer this observation: Jeremiah's "I am only . . ." is a wise response to the one whose very name is "I AM." The virtue on offer in Jeremiah's example is not to begin with confidence in what we know but in awe of the reality that we are *known*. That is why, year after year, I have the joyful task of gently reminding those who come to the work of theology afraid that they do not know enough—that they are not confident enough in their knowledge—that they are likely tapping into a cardinal virtue of the theological life. We theologians do our work in response to I AM, and I know no other way to begin my response than by responding, "I am only . . ."

KNOWN TO SPEAK

In the gracious exchange that unfolds with young Jeremiah, though, it is the I AM who responds, "Do not say 'I am only a boy,' for you shall go to all to whom I send you, and you shall speak whatever I command you" (Jer 1:7 NRSV). Confessionally, my temptation as a theologian is to skip right to the speaking. In all this talk about having words and not having words, I want to get to the point where I have something to say. That is why it is good for me to see the construction of these verses in Jeremiah 1. I am sent to a people, and then I am given words to speak. The work of theology happens in the dynamic of being known by God, situated among a people, and speaking what has been passed on to us. After an awareness of being known by God, we are sent to speak God-words *among a people*. We are sent first. The speaking comes later.

When that speaking does come, then, it is in response to God and in God's very presence. The work of theology is joyful work, precisely because it sets itself up to be known by God and listen well for the words we are to speak. Christian theology is not an exercise in impressive speculation, of dazzling one another with the most novel ideas and propositions about some figure called "God" and that figure's relation to the world. The work of theology is better understood in terms of being known, being sent to a people, listening for the word of the Lord, knowing that the Lord is with us, and then speaking that word.

"I am with you and will rescue you," the Lord says to Jeremiah (Jer 1:8), reminding us that this God is no senseless plant to study or voiceless rock formation, as interesting and beautiful as those are. This is a living God who traverses faithfully with those who are known by God. When we speak for God as theologians, when we say words about God, they are words spoken in God's presence. Theology does not happen as if the subject we are describing were sitting idly by. The work we undertake as theologians is responsive to God. We do not simply say what we hope to be true and move on. When we speak, we do so in a way that is influenced by and immediately responsive to God's own presence, so that when the lines begin to blur between the word-work of explicating some point of doctrine and the prayerful adoration rendered by one who is known by God, theology is probably happening.

"I HAVE PUT MY WORDS IN YOUR MOUTH"

Finally, something needs to be said about the grand promises that conclude this passage. God appoints Jeremiah over the nations and the kingdoms. There may be more going on here than an ambitious young man hearing the voice of God exalt him to such a high and lofty place. There is a very real sense that the one who speaks for God is going to speak to the nations, but using a logic that does not belong to the nations. The words in Jeremiah's mouth are gifts from the God who knows him. So, Jeremiah's speech will not placate the nations. It will speak truthfully.

Around the time universities began to form and theology found a place in them, an odd way of describing theology's function also rose. In attempting to work out the way these academic disciplines, which had never thought of themselves as separate enterprises before, came to work together, theology took on the moniker "the queen of the sciences." An ostentatious title, to be sure, it was a kind of homage to the notion that theology was the study that held all other studies together in this universe that God had created. If the vocation of a *university* was to explore the world, theology was the discipline that was supposed to breathe life into all of those wings of scientific exploration that were meant to tell us the truth about God's world. Mathematics, physics, political science, and the social sciences were all assumed to be in service to unveiling the truth of God's good universe.

There are, of course, numerous reasons this kind of thinking has tended to fall to the wayside in a modern world, and why we should be wary of it. Whether it is our culture's dismissal of the shared belief in God or in any story that links all things together in one overarching truth, or even our modern proclivity to relegate religion to a separate and privatized sphere of the human existence, you just do not hear many folks talking like this anymore. My point here is not to try to claw back the social and intellectual power necessary to re-enthrone theology as the queen of the sciences, especially if its royal objective is to lay intellectual siege to the world. It is, rather, to take a page from Jeremiah, who understood that God-talk could not be relegated to one discipline among others. Nor can the work of God-talk fit neatly inside one of the other disciplines. Because theology concerns itself with the Word of God and our words of response, it will not be satisfied to be a self-contained discipline, speaking only to itself. It will speak to God's world freely.

When God appoints Jeremiah "over nations and kingdoms to uproot and tear down, to destroy and overthrow, to build and to plant" (Jer 1:10), it is precisely because God-talk is not relegated to an isolated sphere of the religious. Theology will speak to the nations and kingdoms, sometimes pulling them down, sometimes building new structures and planting new possibilities. It will speak into situations that may not be overtly theological, diligently reflecting on how talk of the God who is lovingly making all things new influences in *this* situation.

Theologians cannot arrogantly assume that their study gives them expertise in all matters, but it does give a sense of freedom that there is no place where the Word of God does not belong. Whether you want to go with the notion that theology is the queen of the sciences or not, the methodological reality remains: God does not call the theologian to do the kind of work that fits neatly into the preestablished categories. The kind of work theology does is big enough to pluck up a nation, to reduce it to rubble, and to plant something new. Theology cannot be beholden to preconceptions, no matter how comforting or natural those preconceptions may be to us. If it fits nicely into a given category, it is probably not theology. Theology is social, but it is not social talk. Theology is scientific, but it is not science talk. Theology is political, but it is not political talk. Theology is God-talk. Because it is God-talk, it will not and cannot be beholden to anything less than God. So, the theologian speaks with words that are gifted by God. Of course, this only happens long after the theologian comes to terms with being known by God.

Theology is powerful. It is granted the capacity to speak in a way that critiques nations and kingdoms, to pull down the structures of old creation and to plant something new. This is why the work of theology needs to be entrusted to those whose virtuous first instinct is to say, "I am only . . ." This is why it is work for those who know first that they are known by God. I am far too tempted to speak as a theologian in a way that would benefit my preconceptions, to take hold of the knowledge of God and use it to carve out a world to my particular benefit. I am far too tempted to let my theology work as if I were the only one who matters and my perspective is the only one that could possibly be right. I am tempted to do my work as a theologian in a way that benefits me and operates in the comfortable categories that will not leave my life plucked up and torn down. But then, I would be no theologian. I may use words about God, but it is likely that it is not the word of the Lord. That is why I need Jeremiah's virtue: I do not know what to say! I might know how to string a few words together, but that does not mean that I necessarily know how to speak in the prose of faithful response to the divine. Learning to speak theologically means coming to the humble knowledge that I am known by God, that "I am only . . . ," that I am sent to speak among a people, and that what I speak is a gift from God. As a theologian, I do not shrink back from the prophetic truth-telling, but I proceed recognizing that a virtue of the theological life is being known, and the words I proclaim are not mine alone. Beginning with being known helps me assume a posture of receiving and passing on, of locating myself within a long tradition of those who have done the work of passing on what was passed to me (1 Cor 11:23).

The work of theology can never be reduced to support for anything other than God's purposes, and if theology is the work of God's purposes, it may topple nations, kingdoms, or faulty ideas I have held for a long time about God. It may, in fact, topple kingdoms that have been built in the name of theology. But we rejoice at that, because while theology can dismantle, it also builds and plants. Theology is nurturing work, passing on the gospel and giving careful attention to how we can do so faithfully.

It seeks in all times and places to tell the truth about God, God's world, and God's work in the world, so that in all it says, it is proclaiming the good news of the gospel. Theology is not banter about ideas that do not matter; it is serious attention being given to be sure that what we are saying is faithfully nurturing the church in its mission. Indeed, theology can root out, but that is always for the sake of nurturing the people of God. Like good gardeners, the work of theologians is to weed out whatever hinders the people of God from speaking and living the good news that the world is being made new in Jesus Christ. It is bold work, but disconnected from the virtue of Jeremiah, such boldness runs the risk of wrecking the garden.

So, like Jeremiah, we stand in relation to the God who knows, we turn our attention to the way God is addressing us. As we prepare to do our work, our first response is nothing other than, "Ah, Lord GoD! Truly, I do not know how to speak, for I am only . . ."

PRAYER

You have searched me and known me, gracious God.
Before I spoke a word, you were speaking to me, calling me to life by
    your Word.
You have known me before I have known a word about you.
In your mercy, grant that I may find you as I'm being found by you.
May the sufficiency of your divine presence meet the insufficiency
    of my preparation.
Remind me that your Word is cruciformly powerful, and teach me
    how to speak it faithfully.
In the likeness of your Son, Jesus Christ, form in me a spirit of humility,
That I might nurture your holy people as I am nurtured by
    your holy presence.
To your glory, now and forever.
Amen.

QUESTIONS FOR DISCUSSION OR REFLECTION

1. Think for a moment about *how* you know God. What people, events, stories, or life experiences have shaped your knowledge?

2. How and when have you come to know that God knows *you*? In what ways has the awareness of being known by God influenced your theological knowledge of God, or not? (If it is difficult to identify experiences of being known by God, conversation with a seasoned guide such as a spiritual director may be helpful.)

3. Consider the relationship between knowledge and speaking in Jeremiah's life. What kind of theology might be done by those who are known by God first and speak of God second? What would this look like in your own life?

CHAPTER TWO

Jacob

ON WRESTLING

THE STORY OF JACOB WRESTLING on the shadowy banks of a river in the dark of night is alluring because it evokes more questions than it answers. By its nature, it is provocatively mysterious, and that may be exactly why it is also an invitation to the virtue of wrestling with God in the theological life. An invitation to walk the theological life will also be an invitation to wrestle with life's largest questions, with social and cultural issues, and most of all with the holy God who meets us in the wrestling. It is Jacob, a conniving figure in Scripture's story, who invites us to this theological virtue. For him, virtue is not to be found in his upstanding moral integrity; he is the heel-grabbing trickster who de-frauded his older brother by misleading their senile, disabled father (Gen 27:1-46). Sibling rivalry is one thing; taking advantage of your el-derly father's disability is quite another. The theological virtue calling to us from the wrestling story, though, is Jacob's refusal to let go when a mystery lays hold of him. In his riverside work that night, we can see that the call to theology is not reserved for those who always get it right but extends to those who give themselves to the struggle. In the dark of night, alone and afraid, he is overtaken by something he cannot understand or overcome, and still he continues to grapple until the break of day.

There is virtue to be found here for the work of theology, because it is Jacob's tenacious engagement with God, rather than his dubious past, that stands out in the story. Jacob does not try to wiggle out of the difficulty or avoid the situation, a surprising twist for someone with his personality profile. Rather, he embraces the mystery and somehow meets God in the wrestling. In his story, the *who* and the *how* meet on the banks of a river when he is surprised and overwhelmed and refuses to let go.

FINDING VIRTUE IN THE STRUGGLE

In Genesis 32, Jacob is doing what Jacob does. In this case, he is devising a scheme to buy his way into his brother's favor, because Esau is on his way to find Jacob with four hundred of his friends in tow, and he is not happy. Camped alongside a river, Jacob plans to escape his brother's wrath by dividing his own entourage into two groups, taking a gamble that Esau will attack the other group first, allowing Jacob to escape to safety. Sensing the impending danger to his family, Jacob sends them across the river to relative safety, remaining alone on the bank of the river. As night falls, an unnamed and mysterious stranger shows up and challenges him to a wrestling match for reasons we are not told. By the time the sun came up, the mysterious challenger has not only wrenched Jacob's hip but also given him a new name. The writer of Genesis 32 is not clear about whether this man is God, but either way, Jacob is convinced he has met God in the match. "I saw God face to face," he says of this mysterious encounter (Gen 32:30).

As frustrating as this ambiguity can be, I suspect it is a good friend to anyone who has had to wrestle with something in the dead of night while not being entirely sure where God is in it. The frustrating ambiguity in the text looks a lot more like a friendly companion when we are struggling to discern why we find ourselves locked in a wrestling match with something we cannot understand. That may be one reason Israel held on to this story and made sure to include it in the epoch of their origins. Maybe there is a type of theological virtue woven into this biblical narrative that has the capacity to shape who they are as a people, even down to their name. Names, of course, do a lot to shape our understanding of ourselves in relationship to God and others. Being named "God-wrestlers" has to do something to your sense of who you are and what kinds of virtues make you a good Israelite.

Moreover, there is something we see in Jacob's actions on the riverbank that exceeds any virtue we would expect him to have. It is the kind of action that says, "Even if Jacob isn't a particularly upstanding person (and who among us is?), here's what it looks like to respond well to the God who remains faithful." As the story unfolds, we see that Jacob is not necessarily interested in distinctly explaining how the man who attacked him was actually God or how any of that worked. From everything we see in the passage, explaining how a man was God and why he came after Jacob is not really the point, as much as I would appreciate that kind of clarity. Rather, we see that in the struggle, two things happened: (1) Jacob refused to let go, and (2) he became convinced that he met God face to face, and it changed who he was forever. In other words, the riverbank wrestling in Genesis 32 is an enduring image that should come to mind time and again when Israel is overtaken by adversity, addressing how they might somehow meet God in the midst of an unexplainable affliction.

As much as I wish this were not the case, theology often happens in struggle, which means that wrestling can be a virtuous theological activity. While the work of theology often involves offering words about God, that work is usually preceded by wrestling with God. Theology can involve wrestling with an issue, a person, and even with ourselves. In wrestling whatever it may be, we may just find that we have met God in the struggle. Most of us begin working out life-sized God questions while sitting in the ashes of tragedy, trauma, frustration, or confusion. Sometimes it is a decision in front of us that forces the issue of where God is and what God wants. Whether in pain or perplexity, we can, like Jacob, be overtaken when we least expect it by something that is ambiguously related to God. Was it God who caused this situation? Does God want a particular response from us when we are faced with this decision? Taking cues from Jacob, we are reminded that he spends no time attempting to identify whether this really is God. Jacob's odd response is to grab on and refuse to let go, finally concluding that he met God in the struggle.

WRESTLING IN THE DARK

It was not night when I was overtaken. In fact, it was a sunny Sunday morning. I was wrapping up a speaking engagement at a church outside Nashville when my phone lit up. As soon as I was able to return the call, the sounds of raw, unfiltered grief flooded the line. I stayed on the call over the next hour as I numbly navigated my car back toward my house while trying to piece together how and why we had lost my dad in a freak accident that morning while he was helping an elderly woman at his church carry her chair after an outdoor worship service. Nothing about it made sense then, and there is not much sense I can make of it now.

The next phone call I received was from a friend in California who specializes in counseling for pastors. I do not know how he heard what had happened, but his prayer at the conclusion of that phone call was rich in theological wisdom: "Lord, please protect Tim from all of the stupid things people are about to say about why this happened." As it turned out, it was a prayer I needed.

As usual in situations like that, we want to make some sense of it by asking where God was in it. These questions are usually treated under an arm of theology we call *theodicy*, which examines the problem of evil in the world. Did God cause this? Did God do this for some reason we cannot possibly know? My academic theological training offered an array of possibilities if I wanted to try to forge answers to these kinds of questions in this situation. Some theological systems offer a theodicy that states that God's power and knowledge are categorically beyond my own. So while I could, at some level, chalk this event up to God's activity, I would need to trust that it would be for the sake of some benefit I could not possibly understand. Other theodicies offer the idea that God's loving nature simply does not allow God to unilaterally stop this kind of accident from taking place, because a God who is love by nature cannot act unilaterally, because unilaterally overpowering action is unloving by definition. Other approaches fall somewhere in between, making creative theological moves such as turning to the cross of Christ as a revelation of God's experience of loss for the sake of overcoming it all in Jesus' resurrection.

While I do tend to lean toward one of those options more than the others, my pastoral experience reminded me that even the most convincing theological *answer* was not what I needed in moments like that one. It is not that answers are bad necessarily, but any method designed to produce answers—even the best answers—cannot be the whole of what theology offers. As important as theodicy is in the work of theology, if we use it to answer questions about evil, loss, and suffering, we must be careful that we do not skip out on wrestling. In walking the theological life, virtue is not found in having neat answers to the problem of evil as much as it is in wrestling with a painful mystery and refusing to let go through the night of sorrow until we meet God face to face. In the darkness of pain, Jacob's wrestling opened something to me beyond answers. Like Jacob, I had, for no discernible reason, been overtaken by something that I could not explain or understand. Strangely, the longer I wrestled with whatever it was, the more I came to believe that in the wrestling, I met God face to face.

I came away limping, too, because I walk differently as a theologian since then. It is one thing to postulate answers to the problem of evil in theory; it is another thing entirely when you have struggled with God and come away different. Our limp after encounters like those serves as an enduring reminder that wrestling is not some romanticized pathway toward knowledge of God. It is, undoubtedly, a mark of virtue for the one who walks the theological life with a distinctive limp.

I would also like to think that, like Jacob, I got a bit of a name change in my wrestling. For years, I resisted the title of theologian because I was not sure how many degrees I needed to earn before I could rightfully claim that name. "I'm no theologian," I have heard countless people say, mainly signaling that they do not have all the answers to the questions about God and God's activity in the world. It was almost as if one could finally be called a theologian when one had finally achieved all knowledge of the divine. The longer I am at the work of theology, the more I am coming to see that being named a theologian probably has more to do with wrestling than it does about the degrees I have earned or any answers I have. Being a theologian is more about the virtue of being willing to wrestle than it is about the tidy answers we have to life's most perplexing questions. I have, after all, known some professional theologians who seem to walk with no evidence at all that they have wrestled with God. I have also known others with minimal amounts of academic training in theology who wobble along on hips that bear witness to their all-night wrestling matches. "I'm no theologian," they will say again, but their limp tells me otherwise.

The theologians who draw my interest most are those who do their work as a tenacious, passionate refusal to let go of life's messiest questions in favor of simplistic answers. God-wrestling simply does not settle for easy answers. It will not let go, even into the darkness of night, and when the dawn begins to break, the blessing we receive is a limp and a new name: theologian.

> The man asked him, "What is your name?"
>
> "Jacob," he answered.
>
> Then the man said, "Your name will no longer be Jacob, but Israel, because you have struggled with God and with humans and have overcome." (Gen 32:27-28)

Wrestling with God is not an activity God's people engage in on a whim; it is who they are. Maybe we could say the same of those who are struggling to do the work of theology. The invitation to theology is often found in the struggle. Maybe it is more about our passionate pursuit that simply will not relent than it is about having tidy answers to life's messy questions. While theology will necessarily and undoubtedly deal with doctrine, giving careful attention to what we say about God and God's activity in the world, we do so as those who are blessed with a limp. Doctrine is no clean-cut set of answers, sealed away from the messy questions of life. It is the result of generations of God's people wrestling with the realities that have laid hold of them in the dead of night and refusing to let go until the break of dawn.

WRESTLING FOR THE LOVE OF GOD

Many of my friends in high school joined the wrestling team. I was not among them. Putting on one of the tight-fitting uniforms and stepping into public view was a nightmare come to life for a self-conscious adolescent like me. My friends on the team developed a near obsession with making sure their weight matched their wrestling class, many adopting bizarre practices such as wearing trash bags under their clothes to encourage sweating and constantly chewing Skittles to spit those pesky saliva pounds into a paper cup they always had at the ready. The matches were tough, I am sure, but the real battle I saw them fighting was against ringworm infection and cauliflower ear. "So, you're telling me that I can sweat all day, wear Spandex in front of the student body, *and* get a parasite? Do you think they'd still let me sign up?!" I would say to friends who suggested I join the team. Sarcasm can be a subtle art, but there was nothing refined about the way I applied it in response to the suggestion that I join the wrestling team. My wrestler friends, quite simply, had been captivated by wrestling in way I had not. It was something they came to love, and that love drove them to do things that could only be motivated by love.

That was the kind of love that began to be evoked in me when I started to study theology. It was then that I found a love for wrestling. This wrestling did not involve Spandex, a reality for which I continue to be thankful. But when I began to dabble in Jacob's athletic art of wrestling with God, it drove me to do things that could only be provoked by love that was captivated by beauty. From the outside, they were practices that might come off as a bit bizarre. I began to learn ancient languages, grapple with theological texts, contend with tricky passages of Scripture, refusing to let them go until they gave me a blessing. Late into the night, I would read, pray, write—struggle. I am willing to grant that I was doing that in a quest to know the details and doctrines inside and out, but the beauty I discovered was not in gaining clean answers but in meeting God through the struggle. In fact, finding the beauty in wrestling will likely be a key to developing a passion for the work of theology.

Theological wrestling has the obvious advantage that it can reveal the beauty of an infinite God who satisfies the deepest longings and curiosity of the human heart. The invitation to the study of God is alluring in the deepest parts of who we are, but it does not come without some wrestling. Engaging with the divine is incredibly, immensely, and immeasurably good, but it is not always easy. Oftentimes, doing theology is deep calling to deep, to borrow the imagery of the psalms (Ps 42:7). The profound beauty and mystery of a God beyond our categories evokes in the deepest parts of ourselves a passion to want to know the divine. God is an evocative mystery, and our ancestors in the faith have long known that the strongest desires of the human experience go unfulfilled when they are aimed at anything other than God.

This is why an invitation to walk the theological life is an invitation to wrestle. For some of us, that passion develops quickly. Some of us embrace the opportunity when some mystery overtakes us. You can see the glint in the eye of someone who loves to do some theological wrestling. Most of the time, I see it when someone invites me to a coffee shop so that I can join them in the struggle. Often, we find God in the wrestling. Conversations like that can become little Peniels (see Gen 32:30). I can look back to moments like that and say, "We struggled there, and met God, and lived to talk about it."

"Living to talk about it" is a phrase that has taken on new meaning after every theological struggle I have had. When I say that I lived to talk about it, I do not only mean in the sense that I survived, but now that I *live* to talk about it. When done virtuously, theology can become an alluring, passionate pursuit to know more of the beauty of divine goodness. "Faith seeking understanding" is the way many across the ages have described the act of walking the theological life. It is a phrase often attributed to fourth-century theologian Augustine, whom I offer as an example to any who might struggle to develop a love for wrestling, the way my friends did.

"Faith seeking understanding" is a common phrase in theology. It is so common, in fact, that I fear we often fail to sense the passion out of which it was coined. Augustine, a talented young man with a world of possibility open to him, was eventually named a saint, but he did not start out as one. He struggled—wrestled—intellectually, emotionally, and spiritually through most of his life. His *Confessions* reads like an account of the wrestling matches that break out when questions of death, love, sex, ambition, and desire jump us in the dead of night. Among the pages of his prayerful declarations, you can detect deep frustration with his own shortcomings, a demand for answers about why life is the way it is, and a bone-deep struggle with grief, sorrow, even depression. In short, Augustine wrestled, and in the wrestling, he met God. "But you, O Lord . . ." is an equally common phrase in his *Confessions*, often following an account of what plagued his mind, spirit, and body. We could say that the *Confessions* are a masterclass in theological wrestling, especially because they catalog not only the struggle of life but the beauty of divine encounter that evoked in Augustine a desire deeper than he had ever known. Such passion was nothing short of a restless heart coming home to delight in the infinite beauty of the divine. This is the kind of homecoming that contemporary theologian David Bentley Hart refers to as the beauty of the infinite, which enflames human passion and love because we are encountering something that surpasses anything we have known or loved before: "eros and agape at once."[1] Wrestling is not a theological virtue because it makes us skillful wrestlers; it is a theological virtue because in it we come to love God as we are knocked akilter.

Loving God through wrestling, of course, is a particular challenge for those who see theology's questioning and exploration as little more than an unnecessary expenditure of mental and emotional energy that are already in short supply. Theology can be exhausting when that is your

---

[1]David Bentley Hart, *The Beauty of the Infinite: The Aesthetics of Christian Truth* (Grand Rapids, MI: Eerdmans, 2004), 20.

approach, and you certainly will not be able to wrestle until daybreak when that is how you come to the task. I should be clear that there is no argument that will allow someone approaching theology in this posture to have a face-to-face God encounter. In other words, I cannot *convince* you to meet God in the wrestling. But I can offer you Jacob's story in the hope that you might begin to see theology as more than deep thinking, because it is also deep encounter that evokes deep desire for the things of an infinitely beautiful God. In Hart's words, it is "a desire for the other that delights in the distance of otherness. But desire must also be cultivated."[2]

How do we cultivate desire? First, we recognize that theology is dealing with a God who is completely and totally other. The word we often use for this is *holiness*. More than a theological concept, holiness is the word we give to the reality that God is utterly and completely different from anything else we can encounter or study. In a very real sense, the holiness of God is what makes God so beautiful. We "worship the LORD in the beauty of holiness" because it is hard to describe beauty; you know it when it takes hold of your attention and imagination (Ps 96:9 KJV).

When that happens, we realize that theological answers are not the object of our desire; God is. Theology reflects beauty. God *is* beauty. That is, we do not do theology for theology's sake. We do it because God is compellingly, alluringly holy. This means, then, that wrestling for mere sport or entertainment can never be a replacement for encountering God. If our wrestling is simply for the sake of pinning down some intellectual concept, it will likely lend itself to the kind of theology that rings hollow—more on that shortly. We wrestle because of the surpassing goodness of what we find in God when we do. Theologians do not wrestle for the love of wrestling; we wrestle for the love of God. It may be what compelled Jacob to declare that he was not going to let go of what had taken hold of him. It was what gave him a passion for wrestling.

---

[2]Hart, *Beauty of the Infinite*, 20.

PROFESSIONAL WRESTLING AND
PROFESSIONAL THEOLOGIANS

As we will continue to see, virtue can turn to vice when a particular activity is misapplied, and theological wrestling is no exception. As we consider Jacob's wrestling, then, I want to say just a bit on how wrestling might be misapplied in the work of theology, souring from the delight of a heart at home in God to something else entirely. Simply, wrestling runs the risk of becoming a vice when it is aimed at the spectacle of who will win the match. While wrestling can be a means of meeting God face to face, it can also devolve into a spectator sport of sorts, a kind of spectacle in which the meeting of the divine is brushed aside for the sport of entering combat with an opponent. In theological wrestling, the good is in wrestling with God rather than in vanquishing an opponent.

When I was introduced to theology, it was through the clash of titans. Texts were placed in my hands that emerged out of conflict between theological opponents throughout the ages. Augustine went to war with Pelagius. Luther and Erasmus took up their positions in opposite corners of the ring. There are Calvinists versus Arminians, Catholics versus Protestants, liberal theology versus neo-orthodoxy, and so on. In the contemporary setting, there is no lack of those who are seeking to toss their hat into the theological wrestling ring. Competing conferences invite certain keynote speakers and splash their pictures on the promotional posters, a kind of cultural shorthand for which theological angle or agenda that particular conference is seeking to advance. A quick survey of online articles and social media posts also reveals that the arena is filled with spectators, and the wrestlers are ready to do battle.

To be sure, theology involves critique and correction. Whether we are critiquing the work of another or of ourselves, theology is a discipline that trains us to evaluate whether what is being said is indeed the gospel. At the same time, I want to be careful to preserve the virtue of theological wrestling, such that it becomes a means of divine encounter rather than a performance for the sake of amassing more onlooking fans.

Maybe it would help to compare the kind of wrestling my high school classmates did with the type that happens in professional wrestling— the kind that is steeped in performative drama and culminates in things such as WrestleMania. In the first example, there is a type of athletic skill one has to develop. It does not usually have large audiences, and while the teams are certainly competing to win, the coaches and athletes can usually identify some kind of character-forming virtues that come with the athletic disciplines involved. The second example, on the other hand, does not serve to develop character among the athletes but seeks to entertain large crowds, who often have to suspend their disbelief to be able to get into the drama. The skills of the performers are in their capacity to simulate combat and stir the emotions of an audience rather than executing the moves that send a high school team to the district championship.

In making this comparison I am seeking to distinguish between wrestling as virtue and wrestling as vice in theology. If our wrestling is grappling with difficult issues and refusing to give up until we meet God in the struggle, we are likely moving toward virtue. If, however, theological wrestling becomes about how we most spectacularly take down an opponent in front of an audience, we run the risk of replacing virtue with vice. No doubt, a professional wrestling match can be fun to watch, but we are not usually going to turn to a professional wrestler to give us much in the way of true wrestling technique. Somewhere not too deep under the surface, we know it is all a performance that supports an entertainment industry.

Theology can be something of an industry as careers are built and book deals signed on the basis of a particular theologian attracting an audience and evoking cheers for themselves as they enter the arena against a theological opponent. Sometimes you can detect hints of theological wrestling veering toward a kind of entertainment industry, where crowds of people might assemble to hear a favorite voice enter the arena and take down an opponent. But even if one wins the match, has one met God face to face? What was the end goal of wrestling?

Engaging in the work of theology virtuously, especially with Jacob in mind, will call for us to resist making professional theologians into professional wrestlers. It will call on us to resist reducing the goodness of theological wrestling by turning it into a spectacle we consume for our entertainment. In other words, if we want to discover the virtue of wrestling in theology, we will need to step away from the temptation to approach it as aligning with a favorite wrestler and cheering on "our" theologian as they enter the ring against an adversary. We will need to struggle with the nuanced reality that is the theological industrial complex, which often depends on stirring up a group's allegiance to a particular position, naming the gladiators who will fight for that position, and cheering them on as they enter the arena.

Confessionally, having come to see theology this way early on in my studies, it has been a difficult habit to break. It was a methodological approach that could not see the virtue through the excitement of which theologian would call out another by name and critique them publicly. My colleagues, too, were often caught up in the hype of which theological hero of ours would prepare to do battle with another. Again, while the clash of ideas is indeed part of the delight of theology, the question of virtue calls us to ask what point that clash serves. Is it to simply win the day, or is it something more like coming to know God more deeply? Jacob's wrestling happened in the dead of night, away from an audience, and I suspect that is part of the reason we can find virtue in his story. Following Jacob's approach to wrestling may help to demonstrate that theological wrestling serves a purpose beyond bolstering an entertainment complex that plays out in front of an audience who probably knows, deep down, that all of this is pretty fake. Wrestling with life's questions is the virtuous work of the theologian, and the enduring joy of engaging in this work is when, in a surprise to us, we meet God face to face.

BLESSED WITH A LIMP

When Jacob stumbled away from his notorious riverside wrestling match, his stride was marked with a limp. His hip was out of joint, having been "wrenched" by his mysterious wrestling partner (Gen 32:25). Theological wrestling will do that to a person. Candidly, I do not know how to walk the theological life well without a bit of a limp. Jacob's virtue can be seen in that he was messed up in the best possible way, and he walked like it.

I am not sure when it was exactly that studying theology stopped messing us up. I have seen pictures of seminary classrooms throughout the twentieth century, when brick churches in American towns were filled with people, all dressed alike to fit neatly into church society. These were the days when religious education institutions were sending signals to the church at large that they were producing pastors who were going to fit right in. Maybe you have seen them too: photos of young men seated at desks, wearing crisp white dress shirts and dark, skinny neckties, sporting businesslike haircuts, greased to a shine. In these pictures, everything fits. These are the photos that were likely taken to capture the hopes of certain denominations, as if to say, "Look at all these well-dressed, well-groomed young men! Do you see how well-suited they are to do the work of theology?" It was as if schools of theology were where you could learn to walk well, where the oddity of walking differently could be corrected. If seminaries did their jobs right, their graduates would stride across the stage, receive a diploma, and continue walking with effortless ease into churches across the country that were also quite skilled at helping their congregants fit in well to American society.

I hope I am not being uncharitable. For generations, theological schools have done vital work in preparing people for faithful lives of service. I am also not suggesting that a mark of the theological life is to simply offer odd, out-of-step ideas that contradict the historical creeds of the church. Still, an enduring reality of theological education is that seminaries and schools of theology are under near-constant pressure to produce graduates who do not limp. Whether brought about by the pressure to fit theologians in to a cultural, ideological, or denominational mold, or the burden schools shoulder to produce effective leaders, the result will be an inability to recognize limping theologians as gifts to our communities. Worse, we may not be able to recognize an encounter with a holy God as a gift to the theologian.

Jacob reminds us to beware of approaches to theology that are designed to protect us from limping. No one encounters the holiness of God and does not come away limping a little. Encountering God and wrestling—truly wrestling—is going to mess with your walk. It will put you out of step with those who are well-adjusted to fit right in with the prevailing cultural categories. But a theological vision inherited from Jacob can help us see the limp as a blessing. It was the blessing he received when he refused to let go. It was what God provided when he asked for a blessing, and it is what he carried away to show that his wrestling was real. Do not let go. Do not give yourself an easy out. Keep wrestling.

PRAYER

Good and tenacious God,
In a groaning and tumultuous world, we come to you desiring blessing.
We want to know that you are good.
We want to know that you will establish peace,
Even as we confess that the peace we often desire is that
    of standing on our feet,
Being free from the surprise of wrestling.
In gratitude, we thank you that we can meet you in our struggle.
In your mercy, grant that we may find you face to face,
And bless us with a limp, we ask,
That we might walk as those who have been transformed
    by our encounter with you.
Rescue us from a desire to walk as if we haven't wrestled with you.
Give us a vision of knowing you beyond winning temporary battles,
That you may be glorified, both now and forever.
Amen.

QUESTIONS FOR DISCUSSION OR REFLECTION

1. Can you identify a time when grief, pain, or disruption brought on theological questions you were unable to shake off? How does Jacob's story help you think about God's activity and your response in those circumstances?

2. Have you participated in or witnessed theological debates that became a spectacle? What was the outcome? How does the invitation to wrestle with God affect that approach to theology, and how might the outcome differ?

3. Do you find the idea of doing theology with a limp terrifying, liberating, or something else? How might this idea shape your expectations and imagination of your own work as a theologian?

CHAPTER THREE

Sarah

ON LAUGHTER

SOMEWHERE ALONG THE LINE, we picked up the notion that it was not okay to laugh in church, and it stuck. I fear the way we do theology has a lot to do with that, because far too often we think theology is not a laughing matter. I beg to differ. In fact, walking the theological life may have everything to do with laughter. Humor is an overlooked virtue of the theological life. Bursting through the clear delineations of logic and cognition, laughter erupts as if our mind and body are conspiring against rationality itself by taking the mundane, the everyday, even (perhaps especially!) the vulgar and conspicuously transgressing even the thinnest veneer of self-possession. Laughter overtakes us, even when we work to suppress it. Joyfully, laughter resists even the most astute attempts to explain where it comes from.[1] If I am honest, this may be one of my favorite things about laughter. Sometimes, the more you work against it, the more it makes a mockery of your effort. It does not care that you are

---

[1] In his excellent chapter on homiletical humor, Jacob D. Meyers offers five working theories of humor, drawing from psychology, sociology, and philosophy. They are: the superiority theory, the incongruity theory, the relief theory, the play theory, and the affect theory. Ultimately, however, Meyers concludes that humor—especially in ministerial contexts—will not fit into any one of these theories. I am drawing on his conclusions in this chapter. Though my reflections tend toward the incongruity theory informed by an eschatological impulse, the virtue of theological humor cannot be contained or explained by a single theory, pointing yet again to its helpfulness in the work of theology. See Jacob D. Meyers, *Stand-Up Preaching: Homiletical Insights from Contemporary Comedians* (Eugene, OR: Cascade Books, 2022), 62-65.

at your aunt's funeral. When something is funny, it is hard to repress, and most of the time, a venue that is not appropriate for laughter makes something all the funnier.

That, though, is precisely what I find to be so promising about laughter in doing the work of theology. Like the kingdom that Jesus talked about in terms of the plants that grow from mustard seeds, it tends to spring up in places you would least expect it, and it is difficult to stop once it is doing its thing. It is upending and surprising, and it overtakes us when we least expect it. Like good theology, it retains the capacity to surprise and delight, even as it eludes our attempts to grasp it through explanation or definition. Though what strikes one as funny tends to differ based on one's cultural setting, it often intrudes on whatever norms set the tone of our culture and disrupts the expectations those norms call for. Humor often acts like a prophetic critique of the prevailing culture, and it looks most like a theological virtue when it is disrupting the expectations of the socially well-adjusted who want nothing more than the world to fit their expectations. In that sense, humor is a shocking intrusion on the expected, like the kid who has smashed his nose and mouth onto the plate-glass window of the fancy restaurant where a couple is having a romantic dinner and will not relent until they acknowledge his sloppy impression of a blowfish. It offends the status quo and evokes a response precisely because it is so out of the ordinary. Is that not something like hearing the gospel?

Sadly, laughter is a rare companion on the theological journey, at least for most of us starting out. Theology, as we so often hear, is carefully measured and painstakingly selected *words* about God. "Theology begins with God's revelatory word to us," Beth Felker Jones rightly reminds us. "It continues as we respond with words: words to God and to each other."[2] I think Jones is quite right, and this is how I have practiced theology for years. Faithful confession requires the work of theology to devote lots of attention to how God's Word speaks to us and the words we use in

---

[2]Beth Felker Jones, *Practicing Christian Doctrine: An Introduction to Thinking and Living Theologically* (Grand Rapids, MI: Baker Academic, 2014), 12.

response. At the same time, I also want to do theology in a way that makes room for laughter, because the theological life is one of delight, and, as David Ford and Daniel Hardy remind us, "Intense, pointed delight and the explosion of laughter go together."[3]

The full-bodied nature of laughter also carries theological promise. Most of us instinctively know that a spoken "That's funny" in response to a joke, without laughter, really means the joke was not funny. Laughter is humor's way of getting a hold of our whole body as we respond. In a fairly atypical way, laughter is the human bodily response to being overcome by a surprising disruption. (Weeping when overcome by grief is another, which we will examine in a later chapter.) However, the way theology is sometimes done can lend itself to a kind of gnostic disconnection between the mind and the body. Put differently, as a theologian, I have become far too accustomed to issuing a verbal response such as "That's orthodox," while my body goes on unaffected. My argument here is not so much that the Nicene Creed should leave us in stitches every time we confess it but that laughter has long been an overlooked component of the theological life, especially in methodology. Its capacity to shake and move our bodies when a word or image strikes us as funny has something to say about the way theology is done virtuously. That is why we are turning to Sarah, yet another figure in Scripture's story who is not extolled for her moral virtue but is an ancestor in the faith whose capacity to laugh may help us take faithfully virtuous steps as we walk the theological life.

LAUGHING WITH SARAH

If we can learn to laugh with Sarah, a host of theological discoveries await us that rationally chosen words alone may not be able to access. Like other biblical figures, Sarah is a complex and morally flawed person. The virtue we find in her story is not in the way she treated Hagar, dismissing her to take her infant son to die in the desert (Gen 21:8-21). The virtue

---

[3]David F. Ford and Daniel W. Hardy, *Living in Praise: Worshipping and Knowing God* (Grand Rapids, MI: Baker Academic, 2005), 92.

we find in her story, rather, is her ability to incorporate laughter as a response to God's activity in the world. Sarah's giggling response to God's work points us toward a way of doing theology that allows it to be funny in the best possible way. Funny is what happens when absurdity and truth align to disrupt the familiar patterns of what we have come to expect. Theology, if nothing else, is the wonder-filled attempt to say something truthful through our laughter about God's absurdly offbeat disruption of the all-too-familiar patterns of death, oppression, and evil. What could be funnier than looking for God's activity in the overturning death and discovering an old woman with a baby bump?

I remember the day my ninety-three-year-old grandmother announced to the family that she had recently been cast in the church play as Sarah. My sixty-something dad's face lit up. "All right!" he exclaimed. "I'm finally going to get a brother!" The laughter all of this invoked has something to teach us about how we go about doing theology. With a few delightful exceptions, most theology I have read has overlooked, forgotten, or even resisted humor as part of its methodology. The philosopher Voltaire once imagined God as a comedian performing in front of an audience that is too afraid to laugh. My guess is that most of that audience was primarily professional theologians. At first, Sarah resisted humor, too, especially in response to God's activity. Eventually, her laughter became an enduring gift to all who followed in the line of the baby she carried.

The story, of course, is an oddly familiar one. Well beyond the years of being able to conceive, Sarah and her husband, Abraham, receive the Lord's presence in the form of visitors, who indicate that the couple will soon become parents (Gen 18:1-15). Following in the pattern of her husband, who laughed at this possibility years before, and from the safety of her own tent, Sarah giggles to herself at the possibility. Her laughter is somehow known to the Lord, who asks why she laughs. "Sarah was afraid," Genesis 18 reminds us, "so she lied and said, 'I did not laugh.'" The Lord's response, however, does not allow her lie to cover her laughter: "Yes, you did laugh" (Gen 18:15).

The scene ends there. The writer of Genesis does not tell us how Sarah reacted to this clarifying retort. Perhaps the writer wants to let that insistent admonition hang in the air, a reminder to all who have laughed and sought to cover it up. What the writer never makes entirely clear is whether the Lord thinks that Sarah's laughter is *wrong*. Yes, we often imply it. We read negative tones into the text and even count the Lord's inquiry into why Sarah laughed as a type of rebuke. But what if the Lord's clarification came to Sarah more as an encouragement to own her laughter rather than to cover it up? "Yes, you did laugh" could be a prodding encouragement to not let her laughter be muffled by her fear. Laughter may just happen to be a faithful response when the astoundingly absurd truth of God's activity dawns on our consciousness.

IT'S FUNNY BECAUSE IT'S TRUE

What if part of theology's invitation to you was to be brought to laughter by God's activity? This is not to suggest that we make light of the weighty realities theology seeks to describe but rather to tap into the sentiment in the adage, "It's funny because it's true." Too often, truth and humor are seen as unnecessary enemies. Humor has gained the unfortunate reputation of lacking the seriousness that is reserved for truth. Winston Churchill had it right, though, in his clever quip: "A joke is a very serious thing." Maybe that witty remark is funny because it is linking the words *joke* and *serious* when they do not belong together, but I think this is a funny little phrase because it is true. Often, we find ourselves chuckling at something we have heard because it exposes the truth that sometimes gets buried under layers of social convention. Good comedy can often make a profound point by exposing, critiquing, or comparing something we have a hard time seeing. Our laughter in moments like that can be an acknowledgment that having the truth surprisingly exposed can indeed be funny. It makes me wonder whether Sarah's laughter sets a virtue for those of us who might have trouble being confronted by the reality that God became flesh in a politically powerless peasant from Galilee. Maybe the funny helps us see the truth. Maybe theology can be seriously funny.

Christians find the clearest expression of God's activity in the life, death, and resurrection of Jesus. What if the truth of God's work to overcome evil in the world through Jesus was at least a little bit funny because it is so true? If this is the case, I cannot think of anything more absurdly truthful or utterly serious than the resurrection of Jesus. It is not normal for a man who was publicly executed to return to life. In fact, the public nature of the crucifixion is precisely what makes this so preposterous. Lots of people saw him die, but there is no category of normal where we see him come back to life, no matter the method of his demise.

The odd feeling that overtakes me when I talk honestly about what I really believe is probably an indication of just how funny this resurrection business is. "I believe that a peasant carpenter, son of a virgin, from the wrong side of the tracks, got crossways with religious authorities and the Roman government two thousand years ago, and they killed him. After they killed him, he *came back to life* and talked with his friends, and ate fish, and appeared in locked rooms, and generally hung around for several weeks. I think he's God and I worship him." Speaking it out loud reminds me of how preposterous it is, but the truthfulness of it demands that I continue to speak it. When the absurd truth of God's activity hits me like that, how can I say it with a straight face? Put another way, the only setup for a joke better than "A guy walks into a bar . . ." may be "A guy walked out of his tomb. . . ." That, I think, is seriously funny, precisely because it is true.

Funnier still is that the life, death, and resurrection of Jesus is how God has opted to deal with evil, sin, oppression, corruption, and the like. That is a reality that moved Julian of Norwich to laughter. A fourteenth-century theologian, she recorded a series of visions that she received in what became the first book to be written by a woman in English. In one vision, she saw the passion of Jesus as "the overcoming of the Fiend," a reference to the devil. "Also," she writes, "I saw our Lord scorn [the devil's] malice and set at naught his unmight; and he willeth that we do so. For this sight, I laughed mightily, and that made them to laugh that were about me, and their laughing was a pleasure to me."[4] Imagine, if you will, the work of a theologian as helping others to laugh mightily because of God's overturning of evil and to take delight in the laughter of those who join you.[5]

Stanley Hauerwas comments on the nature of humor in the work of Christian theology, pointing out, "A story that has at its center a crucified savior does not invite jocular commentary." He follows that comment with what has become one of my favorite theological sentences: "But there is resurrection."[6] Resurrection is the surprising punchline that makes the Christian life funny. It is a joke being played not only on death itself but also on every familiar pattern in our life that tricks us into thinking that death is the ultimate end, and thus our lives are the ultimate good. Thinking of our lives as the ultimate good strikes me as profoundly humorless. It is completely serious because it has to be. If accruing a bunch of stuff, getting the dream job, or having the perfect house is the real meaning of life, it has to be defended at all costs. If our life is the ultimate end, it is not a laughing matter.

Resurrection is the truth that can make life seriously funny. If it is true that we cannot really laugh while we are afraid, resurrection opens the space for us to laugh in the face of the singular reality that has shaped human motivation from the beginning of time. Without resurrection, this life is all that we have and is therefore the ultimate concern of human existence. Without resurrection, our hope is grasping for and maintaining control. In the surprising event of resurrection, then, the Christian faith enjoys an abundance of life that can join *with* God in laughing *at* death. Pointing to the work of twentieth-century theologian Karl Barth, Hauerwas observes the humor that shines through Barth's work, marking his preaching and teaching with a distinctive sense of playfulness and freedom. "Because Barth's theology was so sure of the

---

[4]Julian of Norwich, *Revelations of Divine Love* (London: Methuen, 1901), 31.
[5]See Amy Laura Hall, *Laughing at the Devil: Seeing the World with Julian of Norwich* (Durham, NC: Duke University Press, 2018).
[6]Stanley Hauerwas, *The Work of Theology* (Grand Rapids, MI: Eerdmans, 2015), 138.

victory of Christ, he was free to enjoy the world."[7] The work of theology can be laughter, if we will allow ourselves to be surprised by the punchline.

DISRUPTING THE FAMILIAR

Churchill was also the master of surprising his listeners by turning some humorless philosophical or political reality into something else altogether. "A lie gets halfway around the world before the truth has a chance to get its pants on," he once said. I think I smile at this because I cannot help but picture some deeply philosophical concept such as truth as a bumbling, bleary-eyed old man, reaching for his trousers while trying to rub the sleep out of his eyes. The oddness of an image like that carries a sense of surprise. I am familiar with old men, I am familiar with pants, and I am familiar with notions of truth, but putting them all together in this way makes the familiar a bit strange.

What else is Christian theology than coming to terms with the familiar being made strange? As an ongoing act of speaking the gospel, theology describes how commonplace realities are being redemptively upended by God's activity. Whether in Jesus' skillful use of parables to flip the expectations of his hearers or the very reality that the wandering woodworker telling these parables is God-with-us, can we behold the surprise that erupts from God becoming flesh? Is the work of theology not to help us and others receive the redefinition of the familiar that takes place over and over again in the history of God's people? Not only does God's activity surprise us with turning things backward and upside down, but also the work of theology seeks to bring these incongruous acts of redemption to our attention. Churchill might as well have taken his line from John's Gospel. If the Word can become flesh, the truth can certainly put its pants on.

The problem is, sometimes theology operates a bit like explaining a joke. Anyone who has ever had the misfortune of having to explain a joke they have just told knows that if you have to explain it, it is not funny.

---

[7]Hauerwas, *Work of Theology*, 142.

Explaining a joke smooths off the sharp edge of disruption. It moves the full-bodied response of humorous disruption into a cognitive space. There is enough theology that has been done like this across the years to convince many Christians that salvation is primarily about what they *think*. Laughter like Sarah's, though, reminds us that God's activity can take us so off-guard that a full-bodied response is exactly what is called for. When we do theology as if we are explaining a joke, we run the distinct risk of shorting the full-bodied response it can invoke. On the other hand, doing theology that maintains the sense of disruption that is so often a part of God's activity might just be what we need.

Jokes are meant to land in a way that catch us by surprise, flipping what we would expect around and disturbing us a bit, even leading to some laughter. I might tell a story of a woman who walks over to her husband as he's holding their eight-month-old infant, looks at them both, and says, "I really want another baby." "That's a huge relief," her husband replies. "I'm glad to know I'm not the only one who's tired of this one." Now, the abrupt turn in expectations and the shock that comes with it is probably what makes that little story a joke. But if I were to have to explain that the father actually loves the child and that parents typically do not exchange babies and that the term *another* signifies an *additional* child, rather than an exchange, the joke loses its sense of disruption that makes it a joke.

"Humor builds on punch-line surprises, disruption of the conventional, reversal of expectation," Steve Wilkens writes, "challenging boundaries, misinterpretation, redefinition of the familiar, satire, paradox, irony, and other related devices."[8] Part of theology's delight is when it does the work of making the familiar strange enough to evoke laughter through reversing expectations, challenging boundaries, and disrupting the familiar. Some of the greatest comedians are the ones who can take common, everyday experiences and narrate them in ways that point out how odd they really are. There is not usually anything particularly funny

---

[8]Steve Wilkens, *What's So Funny About God? A Theological Look at Humor* (Downers Grove, IL: IVP Academic, 2019), 5.

about an airport or commercial air travel until a good comedian gets ahold of the experience. Once you have heard a comedian bring to light how ridiculous the whole thing can be, it is hard to ever see air travel the same way again. That also happens to be the comment I hear from folks in church after a bit of sermonic theology that has illuminated some aspect of God's activity in the world. "I'll never look at that passage the same way again," I will sometimes hear. I only wish they would laugh a bit more when they say it.

This, perhaps, is where we theologians can give some attention to the kind of work we do and get a bit more humorous about it. Landing punchlines is a virtue to a comedian, but why not a theologian? Could we not do our work of proclaiming God's activity in a way that evokes a bit of surprise and laughter? That does not mean we are out for cheap laughs but that we infuse some observational humor into our work that's funny because it is true. We can point out how odd (funny?) it is that God does things such as become flesh, call a bunch of uneducated fishermen to invoke a bizarre insurrection of love that could not care less about acquiring political power because it was obsessed with making everything new, become "obedient to death—even death on a cross," and then cap it all off by being resurrected, disappearing into the heavens, and sending a Spirit that makes folks act like they are drunk (Phil 2:8; Acts 2:13). I like the way Steve Wilkens puts it: "If I started [a] story by saying that a poor, unmarried couple, a group of shepherds, and some foreign astrologers walked into a stable together, it might remind you of a joke."[9] The story of Christ's birth has become so familiar that we often lose the humor of how wildly disruptive the whole thing was. God becoming flesh and being born in an off-the-map backwater, attended by agricultural workers, is enough to make me affirm that we should keep dressing kids up and making this reenact this scene—they both generate humorous surprises. A friend of mine recently offered this amendment to the story: After Jesus was born, Joseph came to Mary

---

[9]Wilkens, *What's So Funny About God?*, 4.

with a basket of freshly baked muffins. "Here," he said, "I made these for you." Mary was puzzled.

"But Joseph, where did you get the ingredients? And how'd you bake them? We don't even have an oven!"

"You're right," he replied. "I did it with God's help." When Mary's expression changed to bewildered suspicion, Joseph finally exploded, "Yeah, do you hear how that sounds?!"

At the risk of explaining this joke, allow me to point out that its humor draws attention to the central surprise, that a virgin would conceive and give birth to a son. The surprise is heightened by the circumstances into which this son is born: poor, helpless, vulnerable, relatively powerless, and still God. The birth of Jesus calls most of the familiar tropes about God into question, and that is precisely what makes it so funny. Theologians have a particular calling to take familiar stories like Jesus' birth and let them be disruptively unfamiliar to us in new ways. I think some very good theology could be done if we heard it in the cadence of a stand-up comic: "What's the deal with the kingdom of God? I mean, have you seen the kind of king God offers us? This guy? And the Spirit— you know it's the Spirit if it's got you acting tanked before breakfast" (Acts 2:15-17).

Doing theology well often retains or amplifies the power of surprise and disruption that bursts in on us when the serious things of holiness do what we would least expect. Theology is a serious matter precisely because it is so funny. It is the seriously funny attempt to speak truthfully about things that are wild, surprising, and incongruous. Sarah's laughter came when God did something that no one could have expected, including Sarah. Doing the work of theology is taking up the task of faithfully pointing out God's activity in the world and offering some observational humor. It is the work of finding words to describe things such as resurrection, virgin birth, healing, new creation, church, forgiveness, and God-with-us. Still, my congregation can somehow confess the Apostles' Creed week in and week out without anyone cracking a smile.

This is quite different from many of our biblical ancestors and theological forebears. What has become for us a matter of logical inquiry, peering back at events over thousands of years of elapsed history, was for them a bewildering set of experiences where the familiar became awfully strange. There are, of course, things such as flaming bushes that do not burn up, dead people who come back to life, and patterns of power disarranged when widows and enslaved girls time and again get the best of kings and rulers (2 Kings 2–6). But what may be even more humorously surprising than all of that is the way God takes old familiar notions such as kingdom and divine power and makes them so strange to us in such surprising ways. We should not miss the subtle humor of God's choice of the runt brother as Israel's king (1 Sam 16:1-13) or the comic buffoonery of nearly every king who followed him. They just could not see that God's faithful and redemptive work was often happening among the outcasts who had absolutely no shot at political power (e.g., 2 Kings 7).

"I DON'T GET IT . . ."

Far too often, we miss the joke. The disciples missed the joke, too, of course. Peter cannot cope with the notion of a crucified Messiah, precisely because suffering makes a joke of a messiah (Mt 16:13-23). Peter's dismissal of Jesus' suffering is a living testament to the reality that doing the work of discerning God's activity in the world without a sense of humor can be deadly to our theology. He missed the punchline: his original notion of what a messiah was and how a messiah reigned was the true joke. The familiar notion of Messiah was made surprisingly strange in Jesus, but Peter forgot to laugh. If you do not get the joke Jesus is playing on the old patterns of power and kingship, reaching for the sword is going to be awfully hard to resist.

There was laughter when it came time for Jesus to be crucified, of course, but it was the old-creation kind, the contorted jeers of mocking, a perversion of laughter's joyful nature. "Then Herod and his soldiers ridiculed and mocked him," Luke tells us. "Dressing him in an elegant robe, they sent him back to Pilate" (Lk 23:11). The robe was an obvious attempt to make fun of any claims to kingship Jesus might make. After all, the familiar patterns of kingly power were invisible in the display before Herod. All they saw was a man whose gangly band of uneducated, misfit followers had abandoned him, leaving him vulnerable and powerless. In their eyes, these kinds of people could only be pretenders to kingly power, and pretenders are fit for playing dress-up.

This is perhaps what distinguishes joyful humor from the mocking sneers of bullies. Bullies can only laugh in the patterns of the familiar. Like Herod, they are keen to detect deviations from the norm and *make* fun of the difference, rather than *having* fun at the novelty of a departure from the mundane. When familiar patterns are overturned, their laughter falls silent. The *metanoia*—the radical shift from old to new creation— will not be a matter of laughter for those who are vested in the status quo. The sound of Herod's mocking laughter is a resounding theological warning to any who make the familiar the measure of what is good: do not be surprised when you do not get the actual punchline.

Learning to laugh at something that is truly funny takes theological vision. For those studying theology for the sake of ministry, this point cannot be missed. Ministry can be a life of laughter when our eye is turned to the joke God is playing on the familiar patterns of power, oppression, control, and kingdom building. If our vision of life in the church is conditioned by the same old patterns of power, we will not see what is so funny about the lowly being lifted up and the mighty brought low. It will offend us. Our laughter may quickly mutate to mocking. Part of the virtuous work of a theologian is to develop "a comical vision oriented toward *metanoia*," a vision of life in light of God's activity such that it has the capacity to transform our lives and loosen the grip of creation's fallenness through the shaking of our bodies by new-creation laughter.[10] The joy of such virtue continues as we offer that vision to others, that we may laugh with God.

---

[10]Meyers, *Stand-Up Preaching*, 23.

Theology in the mode of laughter is also vital for church leadership. When we are in on God's joke, decisions can be made in a way that helps others laugh joyfully as well. Theology without the joy of humor, however, can quickly devolve into a desperate attempt to survive at all costs or a quest to take control. This is probably why the people groups that have never really had much control have produced some of the funniest comedians. Theology that assumes it needs to defend or control will almost always miss the joke.

When nurtured with a theological vision of true humor, the church is a community of laughter because it has long been associated with incongruous intrusions of the norm. From its early days as a kind of subversive underground comedy club, its members would get together and try out new material. They would read out loud texts that conveyed to them what they eventually called the gospel, and it called them into an eccentrically holy life. (Eventually, we called those texts the New Testament.) The gospel was the truthful story that helped them chuckle even as they continued to be pressed out of life in the Roman Empire. Humor is a powerful vehicle for telling the truth, especially the truth a lot of other people cannot see. That is most likely why, as I said above, that some of the best comedic traditions come from people who have been historically oppressed. This is not to suggest that being a member of the church in the late modern West automatically makes one oppressed, but it is to suggest that stepping into the pattern of the gospel has usually made people a bit odd in whatever society they find themselves, and the gospel is then the story that can keep them laughing.

Indeed, the very life of the church is arranged around the odd incursion of the holy into the commonplace. Week after week, the church disrupts the nine-to-five lives of its people by gathering somewhere other than work and welcoming the disruption of the everyday. In taking the time to listen to a sermon, we invite the unruly Word to speak into our daily lives and redeem our living. We hold up the ordinary elements of bread and wine before we feast on them and pray that the holy God would disturb their ordinariness by meeting us in the meal. We even sing songs about the way God has not left the old patterns of power and oppression alone but has subversively redeemed them.

I suspect this is why I hear Mary's song in tones of laughter. Luke tells us that when Mary and Elizabeth see each other, Elizabeth greets her newly pregnant (virgin!) cousin "in a loud voice" (Lk 1:42). Though he does not make it explicit, I cannot imagine this meeting without laughter, because it moves immediately to a song that evokes laughter when you are unexpectedly expecting: "He has performed mighty deeds with his arm; he has scattered those who are proud in their inmost thoughts. He has brought down rulers from their thrones but has lifted up the humble" (Lk 1:51-52). Mary is serious about describing the activity of God, and that is exactly what makes it so funny.

At the same time, Mary's laughter is a bit subversive. It shakes not only her body but the body politic of any system at odds with God's redemption. Her capacity for describing the work of God with laughter in her voice signals that she is in on the joke. As we have seen, though, those who need their own life to be a matter of ultimate concern will hold on to their lives so tightly that they squeeze the laughter out of it. They will not have their bodies shaken. Mary can laugh with God. Herod senses that he is the butt of God's joke. There is a particular challenge for theologians, then, to call a people to be faithful to the work that God is doing in the world such that they can laugh *with* God rather than *at* those who are being subversively faithful. Back to Hauerwas's observations on humor: "Those who use humor to subvert the pretentions of the powerful often have little to lose."[11] My experience in doing theology—pastoral and academic—tells me that those who have something to lose are probably those who have the hardest time laughing with God.

---

[11]Meyers, *Stand-Up Preaching*, 139.

LEARNING TO LAUGH IN TOUGH ROOMS

Doing theology with an eye to humor means that we will need to invite others to join in on the joke. The challenge will likely arise when we have taken faith and its institutions so seriously that we have lost our laughter. Doing work that is faithful to God's comedic material sometimes puts theologians in front of what comedians might call a tough room, filled with those who come with expectations but cannot laugh at any of the jokes. Sometimes comedians face a tough room when their material does not have a truthful edge; the jokes are too vanilla. On the other side, tough rooms happen when the jokes are just too offensive to be funny.

Comedians probably have something to teach theologians here, especially those of us doing pastoral theology. If our work abandons the edgy, surprising inbreaking of God's kingdom, it is probably not worth our laughter. At the same time, if telling the truth about God's activity is simply too offensive for people, that is probably a good indicator that they are not in on the joke and their commitments lie elsewhere. God's activity has always disrupted and unsettled those who just could not find the humor in it, and so the work of the theologian may sometimes mean helping them to get in on the joke by letting go of the commitments that are blocking their laughter. Gifted humorists can do this well, helping us to see issues from unique and unexpected angles, helping us to experience humor where we had not seen it before. The work of theology calls on us to acquire some comedic skill, resisting the urge to offer humorless, bland material that promises the safety of not offending, while also offering a way in for those who may have built up resistance to God's jokes, offended at what holiness actually is.

That will, of course, require that we ourselves learn to laugh first. We need to be able to get God's sense of humor. In my work as a professor, I spend a lot of time with those who are just beginning their work as theologians. There is, of course, the evanescent beauty of uncovering mysteries of the divine that are life-giving and invigorating. There are also plenty of times I will look into the eyes of a student who is struggling to get the joke. It is not that they cannot grasp the concepts but that they are beginning to realize that God's activity is making them uncomfortable. They discover that crucifixion and resurrection are a surprising pattern of being unhanded of familiar commitments. God's activity, authoritatively witnessed to us by Scripture, sometimes even cuts against the concepts of God and God's activity that they have carried into the classroom. Over the months I spend with them, I have come to see my job as helping them to laugh by getting the joke. I do this not so much by explaining how the joke is funny but by introducing them to a vision of the world in which God's activity really is capable of evoking laughter. When we have learned to loosen up from the theological hang-ups that make God's material offensive to us, it prepares us for laughter. It happens in subtle ways across time, in things such as listening carefully to Mary's song and inquiring into why Peter did not get the joke himself. Then I can see a spark of theological laughter in their work, calling attention to it, even if they may be a little resistant at first, in words that were familiar to Sarah: "Yes, you did laugh." And that is perfectly all right. When you get the joke, you do not need to cover your laughter.

Eventually, a one-hundred-year-old Sarah delivers a baby and names him Isaac, which means "laughter." She says, "God has brought me laughter, and everyone who hears about this will laugh with me" (Gen 21:6). Her response to God was not fear or offense. She is so fully in on the joke that she actually invites others to come and laugh with her and the absurdity of her new baby. Her laughter opens space for new life, and her chuckling reverberates throughout generations. It is hard to think of a more joyful way of doing theology than as work joined to Sarah's virtuous vision that anyone who hears about God's work will be able to laugh with her.

PRAYER

Gracious God, teach us how to laugh.

Fill our mouths with laughter and our tongues with songs of joy,

That we might proclaim your work joyfully.

Restore our sight to see how you are surprising us
    with your redemption.

By your grace, grant that we might laugh with you because
    we have seen your salvation.

Restore us, Lord, the joy of your salvation when we have forgotten
    how to laugh at your joke.

In your tender mercy, guide us back when your redemption seems
    to us an affront.

Make us your laughter in the world, to the glory of your name,
    now and forever.

Amen.

QUESTIONS FOR DISCUSSION OR REFLECTION

1. Does the notion that laughter belongs in theology put you at ease or make you uncomfortable? Why do you think that is?

2. Where have you witnessed or participated in theology that needed to control or defend and thus missed the joke completely? What do you think is needed to shift away from such a posture?

3. How do you respond to thinking of Christ's resurrection as a type of punchline? How might this view of the gospel shape your theology and Christian life more broadly?

CHAPTER FOUR

Moses

ON MORALITY

THE WAY EXODUS TELLS IT, there is a very thin line between divine
encounter and moral command. Coming away from the story of Israel's
encounter with God at Mount Sinai, you get the sense that the Ten Commandments are meant to smell like the smoke from the mountain. This
is good news for those of us who have any kind of interest in relating
theology to moral life. The work of theology and the work of ethics are
closely related, but how? Answering that question will, of course, immediately become a question of *how* theology is done—of method.

We turn our attention to Moses now, but not because Moses lays out
a tidy method for relating theology to ethics. There are theologians who
have done this, and we will examine their offerings in this chapter as
well. Moses, though, embodies the kinds of theological virtues that will
help us reflect on *who* we are as we explore *how* we relate theology to
ethics. It is not that we are seeking after Moses' moral virtues, either.
Like the other figures we have examined in this book, he is complex and
flawed, and the biblical writers who give us his story do not seem particularly interested in scrubbing clean his story, presenting him as a
paragon of morality. It is the theological virtues that will attract our attention here, and we will look to the kind of posture Moses takes in relating a response to God to the moral life of the people to whom he
speaks. In essence, we are looking at a man who comes to live the

theological life without overlooking the moral failures of his past, and that is what makes Moses such an interesting teacher for how theology and ethics are done together.

There are, of course, several modern and contemporary approaches to relating theology and ethics that give explicit attention to *how* we do this work. We will examine those and then turn more fully to Moses to see how the *who* might shape the *how*. Some approaches to the work of theology assume that there is direct moral implication that will flow from their work. Other approaches may not have ethics in mind directly but gesture toward certain moral outcomes. Still others argue that the methodological ordering of theology shaping ethics is problematic and flip the script, placing ethics in the leading role.

FROM ABOVE AND FROM BELOW

Karl Barth, a highly influential theologian in the twentieth century, builds ethics into his theological method. Barth's methodological commitment is to be responsive to the full force of divine revelation especially in the incarnation of Jesus and the Scriptures that testify to him, a powerful reality he refers to as the Word of God. Ethics, for Barth, is nothing other than responding to the claim that has been made on humans as God addresses them. "If theology is to include ethics, or a definition of the good in human conduct," he argues, "we must not fail to note that God has spoken, speaks, and will speak to man, so that man is told what is good (Mic. 6:8)."[1]

Barth's "from above" method has come to characterize a lot of theology's relationship to ethics in the modern forms of theology, especially in North America and Europe. His method, however, has been critiqued, especially by those who are working outside the North American/ European context. In the introduction to their coedited book on reading theology from the margins, Miguel De La Torre and Stacey Floyd-Thomas write, "Under the Eurocentric model, theology (what we believe

---

[1]Karl Barth, *Ethics*, ed. Dietrich Braun, trans. Geoffrey W. Bromiley (Eugene, OR: Wipf & Stock, 1981), 40.

to be true about the Divine) leads to ethics (how we ought to act based on what we believe to be true). Theology shapes ethics, as orthopraxis is deduced from orthodoxy."[2] Their description is accurate concerning the way a lot of theology tends to be done in the United States and Europe. Namely, we establish ideas that are true, and then we seek to live according to that truth. Because we are convinced of truth's universality, we often expect others to conform to these ethics as well. We should be clear that Barth's method does not seek to distill ideas out of the Word of God, because for him, the Word of God is the reality of truth. For Barth, ethics is nothing short of the human response to the immediate confrontation of God's Word, so theology and ethics live in an extremely close relationship. Still, this method illustrates an approach by which many European and North American theologians came to *do* ethics: know something about God, then do ethics.

De La Torre and Floyd-Thomas offer another method, however, that they believe to be more helpful, especially to those whose lives are distant from the centers of cultural power. Those who are on the margins, they argue, stand the dominant model on end, beginning instead with action in the everyday world and asking theological questions out of that activity. This method, they argue, addresses the methodological problem of "first order" theological truths not taking the marginalized into account. By beginning with ethics and then moving to theology, their hope is to raise awareness methodologically of the poor and marginalized so that theology cannot be done without them. "This feet-on-the-ground approach to theology . . . not only moves the discourse from the margins to the center, but also provides the disenfranchised and dispossessed with theological perspectives that reveal a God who *accompanies* the marginalized in their everyday struggles."[3]

Methodologically, should we begin with theology or ethics? This is a question that theologians and ethicists continue to mull, many offering

---

[2]Miguel A. De La Torre and Stacey M. Floyd-Thomas, *Beyond the Pale: Reading Theology from the Margins* (Louisville, KY: Westminster John Knox, 2011), xxvi.
[3]De La Torre and Floyd-Thomas, *Beyond the Pale*, xxvi.

formidable cases for their cause. Beginning with ethics, some critics argue, will result in doing what we think is right before we have given ourselves an opportunity to reflect on what is good, opening the possibility of reducing morality to a mere power struggle in which goodness simply reflects what those who have amassed power are doing. Acting first may simply open the door to someone saying, "It's good because I'm doing it." Theological reflection from that point could also run the risk of turning God into an image of whatever our preferred moral approach is, the God who is always approving of what we do because it is an image that has grown out of what we have already done.

Into this valid and vital methodological debate, which is undoubtedly more complex than we have room to wrestle with adequately, I want to offer the image of Moses. My hope in doing so is not to settle methodological debates but to remind those who are called to the work of theology that adding considerations of virtue may help in whatever kinds of methodological debates we find ourselves. In the image of Moses, we find a methodological meeting place between the everyday lives of an oppressed people and the holy God who is with them. His mediating work, carrying what the people said to God and what God said to the people, offers us an image of how a vision of the moral life might be cast, uniting the work of theology and ethics.

THEOLOGICALLY VIRTUOUS ETHICS

Early in the development of the Christian theological tradition, Moses became a figure with whom virtue was associated. Gregory of Nyssa, a highly influential bishop who lived in the fourth century, composed a treatise called *The Life of Moses*. The title of the first section is "Concerning Perfection in Virtue." "Let us put forth Moses as our example for life," Gregory suggests, finding in Israel's story of escape from slavery a model of a person's growth toward virtue.[4] For Gregory, Moses—and by extension Israel—is not a morally flawless person, as we can easily see in

---

[4]Gregory of Nyssa, *The Life of Moses*, trans. Abraham J. Malherbe and Everett Fergueson (Mahwah, NJ: Paulist Press, 1978), 33.

his anger-fueled killing of an Egyptian who was abusing an Israelite. What Gregory finds in Moses' life, however, is an impulse toward constant growth. Like Israel's ongoing journey from slavery toward the Promised Land, Moses continues to move forward into moral goodness. "For the perfection of human nature consists perhaps in its very growth in goodness," Gregory writes.[5]

Along this pathway of growth, Gregory highlights Moses' ascent of the mountain, significant because it is communion with God. Going up the mountain into the divine presence, Gregory says, is akin to entering the sanctuary of the temple, where the presence of God would dwell. Moses' instructions for the construction of the tabernacle, then, are a direct outcome from his time atop the mountain in the presence of God. Divine encounter becomes the mark of theological virtue when it comes to the moral life. Moses is not virtuous because he does not do anything wrong; he is virtuous because he continues to walk in divine communion with the holy God. Israel, then, will find moral virtue in walking responsively to the presence of the God who dwells in their midst.

These dynamics show up in the way Exodus 19–20 unfolds. In those chapters, the presence of the divine descends on Mount Sinai, and it "was covered in smoke, because the LORD descended on it in fire. The smoke billowed up from it like smoke from a furnace, and the whole mountain trembled violently. As the sound of the trumpet grew louder and louder, Moses spoke and the voice of God answered him" (Ex 19:18-19). In this striking scene, we catch a glimpse of a God who is so utterly and completely *other* that the divine presence threatens to destroy the people by its presence. Yet, this is also a God who desires closeness with this beloved people. The holy God of Israel desires to be in communion with the people.

Moses is the mediator of God's communion with the people. In one quick sentence, the scene of Moses ascending into the holiness of God's presence moves to the Lord's word to the people. That is, Exodus shows

---

[5]Gregory of Nyssa, *Life of Moses*, 31.

us that Moses' encounter with God spills over into the ethical life of the people. These two things are so closely related to each other, in fact, that Exodus makes no room between them.

This is the point that cannot be missed: the moral life of Israel is a dynamic, living response to an encounter with the holy, living God. Israel's moral life will not separate *what* they are called to do from *who* is calling them to do it. Their ethical response is not arbitrary; it is a particular response to *this* God, who has rescued them from slavery in Egypt. At the same time, the holiness of this God will not conform to the moral norms of Israel's neighbors. They are to be a holy people, distinct from their neighbors, precisely because the God they have encountered is utterly different. Israel is a moral oddity because they are tilted toward the holy, knocked off-center by the God who is other. Moral goodness is not found in how well they fit ancient Near Eastern culture, but in how faithful they are to a holy God.

Maintaining this distinctive faithfulness, of course, will call for covenant. The way Exodus 19 unfolds shows us a responsive covenantal pattern that helps us understand even more the relationship of theology to ethics. In this pattern, Moses enters God's presence, and God's first word is to remind the people of what God did to rescue them. "You yourselves have seen what I did to Egypt," the Lord says, "and how I carried you on eagles' wings and brought you to myself" (Ex 19:4). Immediately, we see that God is working in and among a particular situation with an afflicted, enslaved, and oppressed people. This is the God who was responsive to the cries of the people and acted on their behalf.

From this point, the Lord offers an opportunity to covenant, in which Israel will become a special kingdom of those who mediate God's presence to the world. Moses takes this offer to the people, who "all responded together, 'We will do everything the LORD has said'" (Ex 19:8). Notice here the dynamic nature of this exchange. God will not force Israel into this arrangement; the response will be theirs to make. When Moses carries this response back into God's presence, the preparations for the formation of a covenant begin. From that point, God informs

Moses that God's own divine presence will descend on the mountain, and all the people will hear Moses and the Lord speaking.

This dynamic, mutual entrance into covenantal life shapes the moral vision of God's people. Its life will be a response to the God who responded to their cries. What God gives them is a word for how they can live responsively to the covenant they have entered. This word is tenfold, actually, and we often know it as the Decalogue (a term literally meaning "ten words") or the Ten Commandments.[6] This is not the place for a full exposition on these ten words, but at the very least we should notice that they begin with a movement toward deep communion: "You shall have no other gods before me" (Ex 20:3).[7] These moral admonitions will flow from being in communion with the holy God. Israel's covenantal ethics are primarily about relationship with and devotion to God. "These sayings live in a kind of spiraling relationship with the people. The words are spoken as description of lives lived in dedication to God, the people live into the description, their lives become more devoted to God, and so on."[8]

What can we learn about the relationship between the work of theology and morality? In the example of virtue Exodus extends to us through Moses' life, we can see first that he is mediating between a people who had been oppressed and a God who heard their cries and acted on their behalf. The real, on-the-ground experience of the people is taken seriously, just as seriously as the divine response. One virtue of the theological life when it comes to morality, then, is to do the same, mediating between real-world realities of those who are being crushed and the God who is coming to the rescue. Like Moses, our response to

---

[6]The term *Ten Commandments* is a heading usually applied to translations of the Bible by editors, but it does not appear in the biblical text itself. Interestingly, Hebrew has a word that explicitly means "command," which is *mitzvah*. The word used in this passage, however, is *dabar*, which can just as easily be translated "message" or "word." The overarching point is that in the context of this covenantal exchange, there is a relational dynamic in play, which may make these moral instructions more of a tenfold message on how to live in response to God rather than arbitrary moral commands.

[7]Among the many sources that offer an in-depth analysis of the Decalogue, I suggest Walter Kaiser Jr., *Toward Old Testament Ethics* (Grand Rapids, MI: Zondervan, 1983).

[8]Timothy R. Gaines, *Christian Ethics* (Kansas City, MO: Foundry, 2021), 79.

God can be one of partnership, even confronting those who perpetuate repression when necessary.

Moses, however, is doing so always in response to God. That is, he is not on a crusade of his own sending. "I will help you speak and will teach you what to say," the Lord tells Moses when sending him out (Ex 4:12). In short, his words are responsive to God in the deepest sense. This is not simply something he wants to do, but it arises as a response to the divine.

We also see an aspect of virtue in Moses' life that rescues morality from the jaws of legalism. For Moses, morality is not an arbitrary code but a faithful reaction to God's holy presence with the people. Moses is the one who will guide Israel in continual and constant communion with God. As he himself moves closer and deeper into relationship with the Holy One, the moral life of the people becomes dynamically responsive to being in relationship with God. Their method of relating theology to ethics, then, is not to devise a clever moral theory and will themselves to live accordingly with whatever code that theory produces. Their moral way is to live in response to the God who has heard their cries, has come to their rescue, and walks with them in the wilderness long enough that they become a distinct, holy people. The presence of the Ten Commandments on its own does not command moral weight; it is only the presence of the holy God that gives the Decalogue its power. When we consider the relationship of the work of theology to ethics, then we do well to remember Moses, mediating between a living God and a real, living people, calling for moral life as relational response rather than rigid adherence to an arbitrary code of ethics.

For theologians who are called and interested in doing the kind of work that engages moral issues in our world, Moses is a helpful companion. In him we find a figure who did not have to choose between "from above" and "from below" approaches, because in his own life and work he mediated God's presence to a hurting and oppressed people, stuck in a very difficult real-life situation. Additionally, Moses did not offer a theory of ethics somehow disconnected from the reality of God's holy presence. His approach was to know and be known by the living God who met with the people at Sinai, and to grow into covenantal faithfulness to that God. In other words, the more Moses and Israel became God's people—the *who*—the more they lived in a way that flowed from that relationship—the *how*. This does not mean, of course, that we do not need to give reasoned attention to how one lives in relationship with God, and that is the work of the theologian. A mark of the theological life, then, is not inventing moral codes to conform to a theory but naming the ways we can live most faithfully for a living and holy God.

SINAI FULFILLED

We move now to another mountain, this one overlooking the Sea of Galilee. It is where Jesus sat down and began to teach the crowd that had gathered. "Blessed are the poor in spirit," he says, "for theirs is the kingdom of heaven" (Mt 5:3). For Matthew and his readers, the implications of what was taking place were amazing. Here, on a mountain, the law is being delivered to the people of God. Again, the presence of the Holy One descended on this bit of land. Only this time, it sat down with them.

"Do not think that I have come to abolish the Law or the Prophets," Jesus continues. "I have not come to abolish them but to fulfill them" (Mt 5:17). What Jesus did next, however, may have put a lump in the throats of anyone who was listening carefully enough to consider the moral implications. "You have heard that it was said to the people long ago, 'You shall not murder, and anyone who murders will be subject to judgment.' But I tell you that anyone who is angry with a brother or sister will be subject to judgment" (Mt 5:21-22). The list continues: adultery, divorce, dealing with enemies. The theme throughout this mountaintop discourse seems to set a moral bar so high that no one could hope to clear it. We can, on most days, go from sunrise to sunset without committing murder or adultery. But that did not seem to be enough for what Jesus was saying. It was not enough to not simply avoid those things. Jesus was calling for a revolution in *motivation*.

In describing the people who would live in this kingdom that God was bringing, Jesus talked about those who not only avoided murdering one another but also had a transformed motivation. It was not just that Jesus did not want them to murder; he did not want them to be *angry*. His moral command was not to simply avoid adultery; he was going after *lust* itself. In other words, while the behaviors seem to be important, what really interests Jesus are the motivations that guide our behaviors. He does not simply want people to avoid doing bad things; he is calling for a revolution of motivation that will lead this kingdom people to not *want* to violate and kill one another. How else can we actually come to *love* our enemies?

Jesus tops all of this off with a staggering moral command: "Be perfect, therefore, as your heavenly Father is perfect" (Mt 5:48). Is Jesus really asking for moral perfection? How can we be perfect as God is perfect?

Though turning to the original languages of biblical passages does not answer all questions or reveal some kind of hidden message, it is helpful in this case. Matthew's account of Jesus' sermonic admonition here uses the word *teleios* in Greek to communicate whatever word Jesus would have used in Aramaic. *Perfect* may be the best word we have in English to get at the meaning of *teleios*, but it generally means something like "complete" or "full." Ancient Greek philosophers would use the concept of perfection to indicate an utter lack of flaw, but Jesus is not a Greek philosopher, and the notion of perfection he is communicating is not about being morally flawless as much as being the fullest expression of what one is. In other words, God is the fullest possible expression of what it means to be God. As citizens of God's kingdom, we too should be the fullest possible expressions of what it means to be human, "the light of the world."

Again, though, we bump into the question of how any of this is possible, and in grappling with that very good question, we remember Moses and the Sinai encounter. What made it possible for Israel to live in response to the holiness of God? It was their encounter with the living God. On a hillside above the Galilean sea, the holiness of God had also come to rest. It sat down, in fact, and began to teach those who had gathered. What makes it possible to live as the fullest expression of humanity? It is nothing short of living out of the encounter with the holy God, the one who Matthew affirms is known by his name, Immanuel, "which means 'God with us'" (Mt 1:23). The presence of a holy God is the moral life-blood of God's holy people.

For Christians, the affirmation of the Spirit's presence with us extends the moral realities of the Sermon on the Mount to us. Jesus was with those people in that place, and now the Spirit is the very presence of God with us even now. The moral life of the Christian, then, is not to will oneself to avoid violating the law. It is, rather, living in faithful response to the presence of the holy God who is with us.

PRAYER

Holy God of love,
We are grateful that in your mercy you hear our cries.
We thank you for our salvation, preservation,
    and all the blessings of life.
Remind us, Lord, of your presence among us, and teach us
    to live in holy response to you.
Where we have created idols, well-intended as they may be,
We ask that you would mercifully call us back to devotion to you.
Remind us that we live in the wake of your holiness,
And set us free to live holy lives in response to you.
Through your Spirit and in the name of your Son, make us to be
    a people who bless,
Mediating your holiness to the creation you love.
Transform our motivations through your grace, we ask,
That we might glorify you by the lives we live.
Amen.

QUESTIONS FOR DISCUSSION OR REFLECTION

1. How would you describe the relationship between theology and ethics in your own life? In what ways can the witness of Moses' life help move ethics away from legalism?

2. Consider the realities of your own context—nation, state, denomination, city, neighborhood, congregation, family. How are you being invited to live out a response to God's holiness either in contradiction to or conversation with these surroundings? What virtues are needed to be the kind of theologian who leads your community in this kind of moral life?

3. Where do you see the correlation of motivation and morality within yourself and/or in others you know well? How might a better understanding of this relationship shape the kind of theological work you do related to ethics?

CHAPTER FIVE

Miriam

ON COURAGE

THE WATERS OF THE SEA had just receded into place, swallowing the world's most powerful military force, hot on the trail of a terrified and exhausted group of newly freed slaves, clinging to whatever they could carry with them. Against all odds, Israel survived their escape. Against every expectation, a vulnerable and frightened people watched the waters of the Red Sea cover up their pursuers, drowning the threat of their swift, violent, and immediate destruction. It was then that Miriam began to sing.

"Sing to the LORD," she begins with tambourine in hand, "for he is highly exalted. Both horse and driver he has hurled into the sea" (Ex 15:21). Her song is short, but it is courageous. With the Red Sea at their backs and the vast mystery of wilderness in front of them, Miriam's song is what sets the tone for these first steps into an unknown future. Without food or water, this people's path is anything but certain. While they may not have certainty about the days to come, they have Miriam's song, singing them into a wilderness journey with no lack of theological courage. Her song recalls the past events of divine faithfulness, propelling them into God's future. I like to imagine Miriam, tambourine in hand, boldly carrying her song of deliverance out into an unknown wilderness. There, between nearly certain destruction and the unrelenting possibilities of danger, Miriam sings. In her song, we find a virtue of the theological life.

THE COURAGE TO SING

Theology can be worshipful proclamation of God's activity in the face of an unknown future. At times, theology is a summons to dance to the hope-filled song of God's salvation. In Miriam, we see the courage to sing of God's activity and dance boldly between the realities that threaten to unmake us. Her life reminds the theologian that our work, in part, is to have the courage to sing of God's salvation so that God's people can dance into the future. It is to create an eschatological culture by staring down uncertainty with a song of God's faithfulness on our lips, calling people to dance defiantly in the presence of possible destruction. It is to step boldly into the days to come, propelled forward by a song of God's past faithfulness.

The philosopher Aristotle famously defined courage as acting to grow, move, or become. For the musician, practicing one's instrument is an act of courage. For the student, courage is found in picking up a book and challenging oneself to learn. A failure of courage, Aristotle argued, was to stay as one was, to be stymied in the status quo. Letting Miriam's witness go to work on Aristotle's understanding of courage offers us a perspective that sees theological courage as the virtue of proclaiming God's actions into the way things are, expecting that God's actions will change them in an uncertain future. In Miriam's case, it is staring down a reality where her people have no home, no food, and no water, and speaking of what God has just done to the world's most powerful military force, bent on her destruction. Her circumstances were real. The threat of annihilation was a bona fide possibility. But the things Miriam saw God do will not let that possibility be her reality. God's activity gave her a song, and to that song she courageously and joyfully danced into the wilderness. When the very real circumstances of our world press in, sometimes it takes a theologian to remind the community of God's action, pick up the tambourine, and invite others to join the dance into God's future.

In Miriam's song, a few contemporary theological resources meet. *Salvation history* is one approach to theological method, made especially popular in the nineteenth and twentieth centuries. Sometimes known by its German title, *Heilsgeschichte*, this is an approach in which theologians give an account of history through God's salvation events. In other words, history is not simply the unfolding of one random event after the next but is linked together as events in God's unfolding story of setting the world right. Some of the first hints of this approach can be found in the Hebrew Bible, especially in books such as Isaiah and the Psalms. There, calamitous events of history, such as the fall of Jerusalem to the Babylonians and the subsequent overthrow of Babylon by Persia, are interpreted as God's divine activity. In the New Testament, Paul adopts a similar approach by interpreting the crucifixion of Jesus not as an unfortunate circumstance of history but as part of God's activity in making all things new and bringing a people to reconciliation.

Miriam's own story can be read in terms of salvation history. Though she is not identified by name, Exodus 2 gives us the story of Moses' sister standing watch over her infant sibling as he floated among the reeds at the banks of the Nile River. Egypt's ruler had ordered that all Hebrew baby boys were to be killed because he feared that the slave population was becoming too numerous to stop a potential uprising. Hebrew midwives, unwilling to follow Pharaoh's orders, told him that the Hebrew women were so vigorous in labor that the babies were born before they could arrive to assist in the birth, a clever act of creative disobedience that was at once a covering to the lives of the baby boys and a dig at the source of Pharaoh's insecurity.

When Pharoah's daughter eventually finds this baby floating in the basket and identifies him as a Hebrew boy, Miriam is there to offer a way forward. "Shall I go and get one of the Hebrew women to nurse the baby for you?" she asks (Ex 2:7). As it turns out, Miriam has just the woman in mind: Moses' own mother. Rather than turn her brother over to Pharoah's fear-fueled bloodthirst, Miriam's "prophetic listening had to be met with prophetic action."[1] We might say that her action is not simply a

---

[1] Kelley Nikondeha, *Defiant: What the Women of Exodus Teach Us About Freedom* (Grand Rapids, MI: Eerdmans, 2020), 81.

clever solution to a problem but an act of salvation-historical bravery;
she is acting in accordance with what God is doing to bring redemption.
"Of course none of this would have been likely without Miriam's bravery.
She may have been a girl of no consequence from the wrong side of the
river, but she dared approach the royal daughter."[2]

As the story unfolds, the baby in the river grows to be instrumental in
God's rescue operation, breaking his people from Pharoah's chains of
slavery. Miriam's courage, understood from the perspective of salvation
history, reflects a faithful young woman joining prophetic action to prophetic vision. This joins her act of bravery to the history of salvation that
was about to unfold. In whatever way she was able to see it, salvation was
on the horizon, and an act of courage turned to prophetic action. The
killing of her people's babies should not be, and she acted in accordance
with an unfolding history of God's salvation.

Contemporary approaches to salvation history include approaches to
reading the Bible as an overarching story of salvation from creation to
consummation. The story, as this approach suggests, begins in a garden
and ends in a garden; the unfolding history of God's salvation is the logic
that holds Scripture's story and our times together. If you want to uncover
the meaning of a biblical story or a contemporary event, then, you have
to read it through the story of salvation history and ask how God is using
that event to work out salvation. Of course, this method has sometimes
been pressed to its limits, and probably beyond them as well, resulting
in near obsession with world events as a kind of historical secret code
waiting to be cracked by those who read Scripture with this code in mind.
Still, salvation history remains a widely popular form of theological
method in many traditions.

Acts of theological courage, then, are made sensible inside of salvation
history. The tales of martyrs may evoke awe or even pity based on the
circumstances alone. But martyr narratives make sense only because
they are joined to the events of God working salvation. Whether the

---

[2]Nikondeha, *Defiant*, 87.

courage of Perpetua, a young mother martyred for refusing to disavow her allegiance to Christ, or Lutheran pastor and theologian Dietrich Bonhoeffer's turn to the Confessing Church movement in protest of Nazism's growing sway over his native Germany, theological courage is more than simple defiance. It is, rather, action in the direction of God's salvation. A virtue of the theological life is the courage to see, among the many forces shaping history, the stream that is flowing toward God's salvation and to move in its direction.

THE END OF THE WORLD

To live with theological courage is closely related to *eschatology*, the theological study of the purposes and conclusions of history. Eschatology has taken many forms in both ancient and contemporary theology, and it is important for us to remember that there is not a single approach to eschatology that has come to be officially recognized as *the* orthodox approach. When we are setting out to do the work of theology, though, it is important to raise a level of self-awareness of how our eschatological leanings will shape the kind of the theology that results.

In the salvation-historical approach, theologians often draw a link between God's past activity and the unfolding of events yet to come. In other words, the reality God is bringing about will be consistent with God's past activity. For theologians who take this approach, eschatology is not as much about predicting forthcoming events as much as it is about recognizing the type of reality God is bringing into being. This also signifies that the future God is bringing will be a good and fitting conclusion to God's previous and ongoing work of creation rather than an arbitrary destruction of the creation God loves. While eschatology does study the end of the world, it often has a keen eye to the fulfillment or completion of the world rather than its cessation. As I often remind undergraduate students, there are two ways to end one's college career. One of them involves withdrawing from school, while the other ends in earning a degree. Both are an end; only one is a fulfillment.

When theologians take a fulfillment approach to eschatology, they tend to read God's activity in history as moving creation toward a good and complete fulfillment of everything God intended for creation. Sometimes this calls for an act of theological courage in the face of daunting circumstances. We might think of the kind of theological courage that fueled Martin Luther King Jr. to proclaim a bold, eschatological future in his "I Have a Dream" speech. In those sixteen historic minutes, King cast a vision of a creation that was more complete, allowing for the flourishing of Black Americans, created in the image of God. He spoke boldly into an incomplete reality, singing a song of what God had done in the past and reminding a people that God's activity would continue in the same direction, that the "arc of the moral universe is long, but it bends toward justice."[3] With the Red Sea of slavery and Jim Crow at his back, King turned toward an uncertain wilderness with a theological vision of God's future that remained unrealized, riffed on Miriam's song, and invited a nation to dance.

Another modern theologian, Jürgen Moltmann, is known for advancing a theology of hope out of the horrors of the Holocaust into a reality where nuclear war remains a horrifying possibility. Grappling honestly with God's seeming absence in the concentration camps of World War II, Moltmann offers a theological account of history from an eschatological perspective. He argues that it is not so much that events are moving from the past into an undetermined future as much as God's future is breaking into present events, especially through the cross of Jesus Christ. In those Godforsaken places such as concentration camps, the yet-to-come reality in which all places are filled with God's redemptive presence comes piercing through the veil of history in the cross of Christ. Wherever one is forsaken or abandoned, God is there in the suffering of the Son.

These approaches to theology exhibit a Miriam-like virtue of speaking courageously into a real situation. Even as we await the fullness of God's

---

[3]Martin Luther King Jr., "Remaining Awake Through a Great Revolution," speech, March 31, 1968.

realized time, theological courage is boldly singing of what God has done in Jesus Christ, speaking it confidently into a world that is yet unfulfilled. The Christian life, we could say, is the dance Miriam teaches us, our bodies moving according to the hope of a God who has acted to bring salvation. In this way, hope is anything but wishful thinking about a favored future reality. Hope, rather, is the Christian act of living now in light of the reality that is yet to come in its fullness. It is looking toward the fulfillment of creation and living its dynamics now because of Christ's empty tomb and the empowerment of the Spirit that Jesus breathed on his disciples (Jn 20). Hope is an approach to the work of theology that calls the Christian community to live now in light of the end of salvation history or, as it is sometimes called in theology, *realized eschatology.*

Tambourine in hand, Miriam sings us into an unknown future, confident of what she has seen God accomplish in the past. The saving acts that rescued them from the grasp of slaveholders will be consistent with the acts that will sustain them in the wilderness, where there is no food or water. Her theological act is singing of God's salvation in real-life situations, even in the face of uncertainty. To be sure, the work of theology often involves proclaiming the goodness of God's activity when we are faced with harsh real-life realities. It is to recall with boldness the activity of a faithful and living God rather than shrinking back in the face of difficult—even seemingly impossible—realities.

PROPHETS AMONG YOU: HOW TO DISAGREE THEOLOGICALLY

Dancing into the wilderness is not where Miriam's story ends, however. We pick up a fuller story in Numbers 12, a complex text that presents significant challenges. As the text presents the situation, Aaron and Miriam begin to question the validity of Moses' capacity to speak for the Lord because he has married a Cushite woman. "Hasn't he also spoken through us?" they ask (Num 12:2). It is a question that the writer tells us the Lord hears, and he summons all three siblings to the tent of meeting.

There the divine presence makes it known to the trio that while prophets do indeed speak for God, Moses is unique among them. "With him I speak face to face," the Lord says, "clearly and not in riddles; he sees the form of the LORD" (Num 12:8). Ultimately, Miriam contracts a skin disease and is banished from the camp for a week. Moses pleads with God for her healing, and the people hold their position until she is well enough to rejoin them, and then they go on their way.

To not shrink back from this text's challenges, let us name them: Miriam, a courageous woman in her own right, is issuing a challenge to a powerful religious leader, who happens to be her brother, so gender dynamics are in play. Miriam and Aaron are both grumbling, but only Miriam contracts a skin disease, so questions about divine retribution and fairness are here as well. Perhaps most perplexing is what motivates Aaron and Miriam to complain. Their complaint centers on Moses' decision to marry a Cushite, a somewhat vague term that usually denotes a person with dark skin from Africa, so at some level racial dynamics are also in play.

These challenges are complicated enough that they deserve more than this chapter can accomplish, but a few words on each is in order. While gender dynamics are in play, we need to be careful to not cast Miriam as a victim because of gender. The writer of Exodus identifies her as a prophet and presents her as a charismatic and powerful leader among her people. Additionally, the seriousness with which her challenge to Moses is taken signals that she could be a true rival to her brother.

Questions of retribution in this text are never very deep under the surface of the biblical account of Israel's history. A general theme of actions and consequences runs through Exodus and Numbers and is amplified in the Deuteronomistic History (Deuteronomy, Joshua, Judges, 1–2 Samuel, 1–2 Kings). As strangely as it rings in twenty-first-century ears, receiving the consequences of faithlessness was the way our biblical ancestors understood the world. God takes affront to the salvation he is working out through Moses quite seriously and is also quick to forgive Miriam.

The questions of race are harder to get at because of what we do not know in this text. Are Miriam and Aaron upset because the woman Moses married is not an Israelite? If so, where was their objection when Moses married a Midianite named Zipporah? Are Miriam and Aaron referring to Zipporah as a Cushite in an attempt to highlight her otherness? Is this a second marriage for Moses after the death of his first wife? Even among the unknowns, the text seems to be clear on this much: Miriam and Aaron are upset about Moses marrying a woman who is "other," and they intend to make this a matter of his qualifications. "Miriam and Aaron began to talk against Moses because of his Cushite wife," the text tells us (Num 12:1). Leaving room for the possibility that there is more than we have access to in this text, notice they are not speaking against Moses because he is mistreating his wife.

Additionally, the writer, or potentially some later editor, includes a parenthetical emphasis on Moses' moral virtue, stating he "was a very humble man, more humble than anyone else on the face of the earth" (Num 12:3). Acknowledging the strong (even hyperbolic) point being made and allowing for the possibility that something more is going on that we cannot see, the text on its face seems to be communicating that Moses' siblings are speaking against him not because of a moral failure but because his decision to marry a woman who is a racial minority among Israel makes them uncomfortable.

There are, obviously, several insights we might try to distill from a story like this, but a blanket prohibition against speaking out when a religious authority figure is abusive is not one of them. This is no cautionary tale against those who would speak out about a powerful leader who is making harmful decisions, because Moses' decision to marry a Cushite does not appear to be harmful. It is a decision, however, that is opening a new kind of future for Israel by calling racial homogeneity into serious question.

That decision apparently stirred up discomfort among Miriam and Aaron and raised questions of how the theological virtue of courage could quickly sour into a vice. In this moment, the courageous impulse that drove Miriam to sing her way into an uncertain future begins to be turned against Moses, who is ushering in a new future by marrying an outsider. The old-creation realities of slavery, death, and destruction are no longer the rivals against which Miriam proclaimed her song. Now, Moses becomes the target of her zeal.

What, then, makes the difference between virtue and vice when it comes to courage? Courage is a theological virtue when it is aimed at the faithful proclamation of the gospel and the eschatological hope the gospel brings. Courage becomes a vice when it is aimed at bringing down the prophets who are ushering in God's redemption. Wisdom calls us to humbly remember that the same person who can employ courage virtuously may also at times use it erroneously. How could the girl hiding among the reeds at the Nile's shore, who acted prophetically on behalf of God's future and grew into a woman with a prophetic gift of singing God's future, turn her courage into an attack against Moses when he included an outsider?

Perhaps our time is better spent asking whether we see ourselves reflected in this story. Has a gift of speaking and acting prophetically been turned against those who now welcome God's future because that inbreaking reality disquiets and unsettles us? Has the theological courage of our past turned from virtue to vice? Theologians have an exhilarating calling to sing and dance into God's faithfulness, leading the people in the rhythms of those who boldly live an eschatological life. And yet, it is all too common that the first ones to call a prophet's qualifications into question are fellow theologians who are feeling uncomfortable.

DISCERNING COURAGE

Discerning our use of courage is always done in the face of the reality that we, like Miriam, are susceptible to using our voices in ways that miss the mark of proclaiming the gospel faithfully. Stewarding the theological virtue of courage calls us to bravely articulate an eschatological vision of God's future, embodied in the crucified and resurrected body of Jesus

Christ and empowered by the Holy Spirit. The future theologians bravely name is not a preferred hope of our own invention but the reality that is arriving in the life, death, and resurrection of Jesus. That future, of course, will be at odds with the way things are, and developing the theological virtue of courage calls us to wisely discern whether our boldness is in service to the gospel or some other agenda.

This kind of discernment can often happen in the company of other theologians, who can point out when our work is straying from our purpose. The voices of others can become a vital gift as we evaluate whether our courage is carrying us toward faithfulness. Their perspectives can help our own work along in aiding us to see unintended consequences and the like. Sometimes, of course, the voices of others speak in terms of critique, and on this point it is important to remember that theology works best when we critique others as an act of discernment so that we might both discover a more faithful pathway. Critiquing others merely for the sake of winning an argument moves us closer to Miriam's misstep. Faithful critique, however, can be a gift, even if it feels like conflict.

The theological life will not be absent of conflict, nor should it. Conflict has been a necessary vehicle for developing the wisdom of discernment from the church's earliest days. Whether it be Arius against Athanasius, Augustine against Pelagius, or Luther against Zwingli, these pressure-filled clashes have been the tectonic collisions out of which the canon of the Bible and the very shape of orthodoxy have emerged. Returning to Athanasius as a famous fourth-century example, he was concerned that fellow theologian Arius's account of Jesus contained a flaw so fatal that the gospel of God's incarnation was dismantled. If Jesus were not fully God and fully human, Athanasius argued, not only would he not be worthy of our worship, but he also could not open to us the fullness of God's future. Arius's denial of Jesus' full divinity ran the risk of making Jesus an influencer of history, perhaps, but not the one through whom the fullness of salvation history was being made present. In short, Arius's claim that Jesus was higher than average humans but lower than God short-circuited the eschatological importance of his life, death, and resurrection.

The decisions that took place at Nicaea are not the absolute model for virtuous discernment. In the wake of the council, some theologians made Arius himself the problem, setting him up as a rival to be vanquished. At the same time, we can also see their insistence that it would be too trifling a thing for Athanasius to win the argument for the sake of overcoming a rival. What was at stake was the silencing of Miriam's song. In short, if Arius's position were to have won the day, the church's eschatological song would not be much of an anthem. If Jesus were not really the fullness of God, how could his followers join in chorus with Miriam, bravely proclaiming God's victory over death and slavery? Jesus would be just another guy, and history would go on subject to the pharaohs, who would employ tactics such as the killing of babies to maintain their grasp on history. No, if Jesus were not fully God, his crucifixion and resurrection would not be the chain-breaking reality on which all of salvation history turns. "He, the risen Jesus," John Webster reminds us, "the new (counter-) creation, *is* the presence of the eschaton, and it is because of him that Christian culture is eschatological."[4]

We need to make this much clear: *theological virtue is aimed at faithfulness to God's future rather than winning an argument.* In the case of Athanasius and Arius, the ultimate objective was not to win the argument but to find the words that most faithfully announce how God is acting in the world.

This distinction, I fear, gets lost in many contemporary fights around issues of theology. Too often we enter theology surveying the landscape of different methodologies and approaches as a battlefield. I can recall seeing a sarcastic message posted online about how to get into theology. "Choose a position as early as you can in your theological development," it said. "Identify those who espouse that position, befriend them, and make all others your enemies." The trouble with this message is that for

---

[4]John Webster, *The Culture of Theology*, ed. Ivor J. Davidson and Alden C. McCray (Grand Rapids, MI: Baker Academic, 2019), 53.

the first five years of my theological study, I would not have picked up on the sarcasm. In short, that was simply the way theology was presented to me as I was beginning to study. Rival theologians were taking up opposing positions in enemy camps, and as I understood it, my job was to quickly find my place and identify my own rivals.

Taking Miriam as a teacher, I would rather join her song than echo her accusation against Moses. I would rather aim my courage toward the proclamation of God's faithfulness than at a perceived rival. When theologians bring arguments against one another, then, our hope is that we can hear Miriam's song in the background and call the church to join it in her spirit of courage. Our motivation is not simply to win the argument over a rival but to free the church to lyrically proclaim the goodness of the God who has thrown horse and driver into the sea and to dance into the future that is opening to us. Embodying the theological virtue of courage sharpens our language, not as an instrument of victory over rival theologians but as an instrument of praise for the God who has brought victory over the ultimate rivals of sin and death.

The exhilarating work of theology, then, is to help the Christian community to sing with Miriam and dance into God's future. It is to take tambourine in hand and join the song. There will, of course, be those along the way with whom we disagree, but a *virtue* of courage reminds us that we need not call their theological capacity into question because they make us uncomfortable or represent a disruption to the status quo. Virtuous courage will ask whether their work is helping people sing the song of God who brings salvation or rather introducing a verse that upholds old creation and its pharaohs. To return to John Webster's vibrant description, "Christian eschatological culture is a place where God's overthrow of sin attains a special visibility."[5] Will we, as theologians, have the courage to make God's overthrow not only visible but audible? Is our courage aimed at helping guide the people in

---

[5]Webster, *Culture of Theology*, 54-55.

singing the song of salvation, or will we distract ourselves by merely attacking rivals in yet another attempt to steer history toward our favored outcome, using a diminished form of theology as our tool?

For several years in my young adulthood, I had the joyful opportunity to worship with a group of Christians in southeast San Diego, where the old-creation realities of oppression, violence, and poverty were as real as Pharoah's grasp on Israel. Losing a friend to gang violence was not a societal issue to most of the members of our youth group, because it was their lived reality. A house directly behind our building had been used as a den of addiction for years, and it was not completely uncommon to arrive at the church building on a Sunday to find new bullet holes puncturing the façade from the night before.

Our worship, week after week, was an act of theological courage. I do not mean that we congratulated ourselves on not abandoning the neighborhood in favor of a tidy, suburban location with a lower crime rate. I also do not mean that we cheered on the advancement of our theological positions over those of vanquished rivals. I mean this in the sense that for many in our congregation, gathering to sing the refrains of God's goodness was courageous in the face of a world that threatened to hold them in addiction, homelessness, or any other number of hallmarks of a fallen creation. But we sang. "In the name of Jesus, in the name of Jesus, we have the victory! In the name of Jesus, in the name of Jesus, Satan will have to flee! Tell me, who can stand before us, when we call on his great name? Jesus, Jesus, precious Jesus, we have the victory!"[6] On our way to Communion each week, we would gather as Christ's body around the Lord's table and celebrate the salvation history that was breaking out in our neighborhood. While each person was served, we sang some more. "Victory is mine, victory is mine, victory today is mine! I told Satan, get thee behind, victory today is mine!"[7]

---

[6]Walter Owens, arr., "In the Name of Jesus," in *African American Heritage Hymnal* (Chicago: GIA, 2000), 303.

[7]Dorothy Owens and Alvin Darling, "Victory Is Mine," in *African American Heritage Hymnal*, 489.

Those brave refrains were utterly and courageously eschatological. Proclaiming the reality of what God has already done in Jesus gave us a capacity to sing them into a situation where all had not yet been completed. Yet, Christ's body was eschatologically formed in our gathering. They may not have been Miriam's words precisely, but I think we were singing in her voice.

PRAYER

Mighty God of our salvation,
We sing to you, for you are highly exalted.
Both horse and driver you have hurled into the sea.
You have rescued us from the hands of those who would crush us
    to make their kingdom great
And have set us free for your holy purposes.
In your mercy, teach us to be courageous because of you.
With your servant Miriam, teach us to sing of your hope
    in an uncertain world.
Guide our courage, we ask. By your Spirit and in the name of your Son,
Direct our courage toward the proclamation of your goodness
And forgive us when we turn against each other.
Give us a common life, Lord, that is a prophetic proclamation that you
    are making all things new,
That in our lives, you would receive glory and honor, now and forever.
Amen.

QUESTIONS FOR DISCUSSION OR REFLECTION

1. Consider how you might identify with the two parts of Miriam's story. Can you recall a time you embodied theological courage by taking action in the direction of God's salvation? Has your courage ever been turned against other theological voices? What was the difference within you during these two scenarios?

2. How would you characterize the kind of future God is bringing? How does this understanding of eschatology form you toward courage and shape your theological work?

3. Which women and men serve as exemplars of theological courage for you? How do their lives and work challenge you to embody the virtue of courage yourself?

CHAPTER SIX

Isaiah

ON BEING UNDONE

ISAIAH'S PASSION FOR HIS PEOPLE flows through his prophetic proclamations. His is the heart of one who loves ever so deeply, the heart of a man who longs for his people to step off the pathway toward destruction and onto the pathway toward life. There is a pulse-quickening urgency in his message: life will only be found in communion with the Holy One. "If we have any hope of being who we've been called to be," Isaiah calls out to his beloved people, "it will be in decisively rejecting anything other than the God who is utterly and completely holy." Communion with the Holy One is the lifeblood of the people, the connection that enlivens their capacity to be a blessing to the nations. "We are who we are because of who our God is," you can imagine Isaiah saying, his voice brimming with zeal.

His message was not one about some theological theory. His prophetic word-work gushes from his experience of his own encounter with holiness, a vivid vision he recounts in which he was suddenly and unexpectedly caught up into God's very presence. These are the kinds of encounters that words cannot capture adequately, but like so many who have done the work of theology, we cannot help but try. Isaiah employs the best description he can find: "I saw the Lord, high and exalted, seated on a throne; and the train of his robe filled the temple" (Is 6:1). A temple filled to excess with the divine presence, smoke filling the room, heavenly creatures flying and singing their praise, an altar prepared for an offering—all of these intense and brilliant images come together in what Isaiah can only describe as seeing God.

The prophet's reaction is immediate, instinctual, even primal. "Woe to me!" he cries out. "I am ruined! For I am a man of unclean lips, and I live among a people of unclean lips, and my eyes have seen the King, the LORD Almighty" (Is 6:5). This is not the kind of thing you can prepare yourself to experience; there are no words on hand for just such an occasion. Isaiah's reaction tumbles out of his unclean lips, raw and unfiltered. It is just what happens when you encounter the Holy One. It is what happens when you are undone by beauty that bursts the seams of even the most ornate description. Beauty, after all, does not lend itself to clean descriptions or once-and-for-all definitions. You know beauty when it stuns you; you know the beauty of holiness when it undoes you. It is knowledge that rages against our attempts to catalog it in a definition and contain it in a theological dictionary. From the beginning, we get the distinct sense that the knowledge Isaiah will gain in this encounter will not lend itself to some quixotic quest to have all the answers *about* God; this is knowledge that will transform Isaiah into the kind of person who speaks *for* God.

One of the heavenly creatures flies to Isaiah with a live coal, taken with care from the hot altar in the temple, pressing it to Isaiah's lips. "See, this has touched your lips; your guilt is taken away and your sin atoned for," Isaiah hears (Is 6:7). It is then and only then that this newly minted prophet is prepared to speak God-words. To the Lord's question, "Whom shall I send?" Isaiah lets loose with another immediate response: "Here am I. Send me!" (Is 6:8).

When the smoke clears from this stunning vision, theological virtue begins to come into view. In Isaiah, we find a response fitting for a prophet in the making, and the one who will speak for God begins by encountering the holiness of the one sending him. There is nothing of defensiveness in Isaiah's posture. He has not entered the divine throne room to plead the case of his people. Rather, he simply and immediately confesses, unhanding anything he might be tempted to hold in resistance. He does not make a case for his qualifications. When encountering the absolute otherness of the Holy One, what case could he possibly make? His virtue is in responding confessionally, allowing this encounter to change who he is, which will ultimately shape the kind of work he does.

While he quickly confesses his own contamination, his people's is close behind. Isaiah will not blame them because he is one of them. His theological work will be defined by being encountered by the Holy One and passionately speaking to his people out of the overflow of this encounter. Smelling of holy smoke, with burns on his lips and the song of the creatures' worship in his ears, he stands with and among his own time, his place, and his people, sent to proclaim the goodness of God and the emptiness of idols. Isaiah does not extract himself from his idolatrous and foolish people, nor does he shake off an encounter with the Holy One. At this intersection we find rich virtue for the theological life.

BEING UNDONE

"I am ruined!" is not something we expect someone to say when something good is taking place. It is, however, the only thing Isaiah can seem to say when he is encountered by God. "Being undone" is how some translations put this destabilizing exclamation. It is a phrase that can be read in different ways with a different tone each time our eyes fall on it. On one pass, it may be Isaiah lamenting. On another it may be a breakthrough of discovery. Often, in the theological life, both are happening at the same time. There is virtue to be found here, because the undoneness of a person is a signpost of theological virtue.

Being undone can be thrilling and disorienting at once, and when in the presence of holiness, we should not expect anything less. It is now time to say it simply: studying theology will ruin you. It will not leave your comfortable categories intact. If theology includes an encounter with the holy God, your lips will be burned. Some of the foundational ideas on which your life has been built may be shaken like the temple of Isaiah's encounter. You may find that, in comparison to the

holiness of God, your people have unclean lips, and you too are con-
taminated. But when theology is done well, this is not where the
journey ends. The encounter with God is not meant for destruction or
deconstruction alone but to be able to send one who will speak faithfully for God. In fact, even our understanding of knowledge is apoca-
lyptically shattered in this kind of encounter. Knowledge now is not
merely having the answers for the sake of having answers and winning
arguments. In the presence of holiness, there is transformation; even
knowledge now starts from a place of raw honesty about our unclean
lips and the goodness of God. When Isaiah's encounter is complete, he
is not destroyed but commissioned to speak for God. The threat of his
destruction has become a means of virtue.

By no means does saying this make the journey simple or easy. I have
looked into the eyes of too many students across the years, some
brimming with tears, as the walls of the temple begin to shake under
their feet. Ideas they have carried with them about who God is begin to
feel empty in their hands as they give themselves to encountering the
Holy One. Sometimes, their hands tremble as they release what they have
come to realize is an idol.

Idolatry is a word that might ring harshly in our ears, but I do not use
it here to inflict guilt or use shame as an educational tool. I use it acknowledging that the idols Isaiah's own people were used to using were
not so much actively evil as they were inert. Made of wood or stone, they
simply sat there, doing nothing. They may have held artistic or senti-
mental value, and in fact they may been quite beautiful, but they were
not the living God who filled the temple to overflowing. Here, then, is
where theological virtue is to be found: in releasing the idols we have
worshiped in favor of the Holy One. The beginning of theological virtue
for Isaiah is an encounter that allows him to confront the idolatry of his
people. Theological vice can be clinging to idols—even ideas we have
about God—we refuse to release. These are often deeply held and well-
intentioned beliefs, but if we do not release them, what kind of theologians will we be?

Isaiah's life is a reminder that no idol compares to the Holy One. Theologians are undone people, ruined by an encounter with the Holy One, called to speak with burned lips to their people of the liberating freedom that comes from doing the hard work of letting go of our wood and stone.

IDOLS WILL DISAPPEAR

The seductive temptation to make our own ideas and experiences into idols is one that the theologian must confront time and again. Yet, theologians who forget Isaiah's theological virtue also run the risk of presenting a set of ideas that is so pristinely disconnected from the churning grist of everyday life that their thoughts are little more than an idol of wood or stone, deaf to the songs of a people's celebrations, blind to the suffering of the oppressed, and equally inert in the world's history.

This is the kind of idolatry, in fact, that is never far from Isaiah's mind. These people, the people who have raised him and among whom he has made his home, are consumed with the worship of idols. More than a finger-wag in response to the violation of some rule, the prophecy Isaiah issues forth speaks to the very heart of the matter: "The LORD Almighty has a day in store for all the proud and lofty. . . . The LORD alone will be exalted in that day, and the idols will totally disappear" (Is 2:12, 17-18). In essence, idolatry moves the attention of the people away from a living God who acts and instead toward inert objects that do nothing. As the prophet knows, centering worship on a piece of wood will have consequences for the people. The result is being cut off from the dynamic, living relationship that makes them who they are as a people.

Perhaps, then, this is why Isaiah's vivid call to speak is so memorable. With the vision of a holy God having shaken him to his core, Isaiah's immediate reaction is to cry out, "I am ruined! For I am a man of unclean lips, and I live among a people of unclean lips, and my eyes have seen the King, the LORD Almighty" (Is 6:5). In an instant, Isaiah knows that he is not going to be able to disentangle himself from his people and their sin. His instincts here press to us an important question: Does our theological work take our own situation among an unfaithful people into serious account? What kind of theology will I really be able to do if I dive into the work as if nothing is wrong in my context or even with my people? Is there a temptation I am facing to do my work as a theologian by extracting myself from my people and their shortcomings, or am I really willing to speak among them as one of them, acknowledging that I remain entangled in a web we share?

Modern theologians often experience pressure to distance themselves from their people when that people's foibles are exposed under the bright light of divine holiness. Some theologians may choose to jettison the moniker that ties them to a people, to shed the husk of a name that links them to a tradition or community when that community's idolatry comes to light. While there can be reasons for theologians needing to move on, we also must acknowledge the crouching temptation. Moving on can be a means of giving us a place outside the people from whom we might be able to issue our prophetic critiques, letting the people become a "them" from whom we have been extracted.

Isaiah, however, affords himself no such extraction. His unclean lips must be acknowledged alongside the unclean lips of his people. He is in this with them. He is honest about his people, his situation, and his placement in all of it—*and he is undone by it.* To be more specific, he is undone by encountering the absolute otherness of a holy God and acknowledging his own embeddedness in a community that has failed to live up to its calling.

Encountering a holy God redemptively rips away any pretense Isaiah brings about his people. Yes, they are his people, but when faced with true holiness, he does not issue a word of defense on their behalf. Isaiah does not attempt to excuse them or ask God to overlook their unfaithfulness. He does not attempt to preserve anything that has come to define Judah's collective life, cultural, nostalgic, or otherwise. He is simply *undone* by God as a member of his people. Holiness disorients and reorients, helping us to let go of the things to which we cling, even when those things are central to our people.

Adopting Isaiah's theological virtue may save us a long, empty, idolatrous journey under the guise of doing theology. His example may help us to be honest about what we are carrying into the work of theology and to confess that the temptation to use theology to defend what we happen to prefer is always lurking. If we theologians are going to be free to do the work of theology, placing ourselves in a posture of encountering holiness will become a necessary part of our work. This may not mean that we have a throne-room encounter every morning, but the consistent formation that comes with prayer and worship can often move us away from doing theology as a means of defending our favorite theological positions or points of cultural privilege.

Theology is the act not of defending a position but of free response to God. Carrying around commitments that are more important to us than God will only hinder our freedom as theologians. Any theological position that becomes more important than responding to God is most likely an inert idol that is merely taking up space in our hands. Because our work is done in response to a holy God, we are obligated to hold loosely to all theological positions and cultural commitments. They may be commitments that are dear to our people, but the moment we refuse to release them in our encounter with holiness is the moment we know they have become idols. Isaiah's words are an enduring and freeing reminder to all who seek to do theology: "I am undone!"

From Isaiah, we find this sign of virtue: preparing to speak God-words amid a people may mean being undone when we encounter God as a member of that people. This is a taxing reality that does not need to end in destruction, however. Generations of theologians have followed in Isaiah's footsteps, acknowledging their place among a community that is losing its way and speaking a redemptive word among that people. Being undone with that people, though, is Isaiah's prerequisite to speaking.

SON OF AMOZ

Every theologian works from within a network of contextual realities. Our people, our time, our situation—all of it comes to shape the way we receive, interpret, and respond. The Jerusalem prophet Isaiah does not shirk his context for a moment.[1] Situating his work among a particular people and in response to particular events, he issues forth God-talk that gives us a vision for how theologians work *among* a people and *in* a context.

Isaiah's God-words are a unique gift among those in the biblical canon, especially for those who approach them with an eye to the way those words work. Three distinct tributaries flow together to form the River Isaiah. There is the first stream, bubbling with confidence in the Lord's ability to uphold the holy city Jerusalem, even under threat from nearby enemies. That stream eventually joins with the distinctive flow of theological words meant to comfort those who are sitting in the rubble of Jerusalem's utter destruction at the hands of the Babylonians. Finally, a third rivulet joins its message as returning exiles find that their homecoming is not as glorious as they had hoped and that life in the land is exceedingly hard. Isaiah is, in one book, a study in speaking to a people of God's activity in very different seasons of life.

This is not to say that theological method is nothing more than the acquired skill to match a message to a situation. Isaiah's prophecy demonstrates something richer than reaching into a grab bag of theological sentiments and pulling out just the right one for "such a time as this." On display in these oracles is an ability to recognize and speak of divine activity in the gamut of the life of a people, from relative stability and calm to the complete disorientation and devastation of life shattered into shards.

Isaiah's prophecy also represents the tension of speaking of God when treasured theological commitments are ripped away. The confident hope that the Lord would not let Jerusalem fall came to a hard reckoning as Babylonian soldiers forcibly carried away the defeated residents of the holy sanctuary. In the words of the prophet, we see how one might go

---

[1]Scholarly consensus is that the book of Isaiah is an amalgamation of two or three works, possibly written by different prophets. While I will not ignore this reality, I am going to focus on the themes that hold the book together, lifting out points of reflection for the work of theological method.

about the work of speaking of God when even the most basic of our theological presuppositions have been shaken.

Overall, though, Isaiah highlights how the work of theology can embody the virtue of being responsive to a people in a place, even as they are experiencing very different seasons of life. There are no easy theological fallbacks here. The prophets who speak for God cannot rest on tired clichés. The work of theology calls for much, much more. It calls for speaking to a people who are walking through this, and doing so truthfully.

Attempting to lift Isaiah's context and drop it onto ours for the sake of learning something about theological method would probably present too many challenges to be very useful. His people were his people. His issues were his issues. At the same time, Isaiah's virtuous posture—his relational situatedness—to his people and their history opens to us an image of the theologian at work.

"Hear me, you heavens! Listen, earth! For the LORD has spoken," Isaiah begins (Is 1:2). These opening words to his prophetic work are historically situated; this is "the vision concerning Judah and Jerusalem that Isaiah son of Amoz saw during the reigns of Uzziah, Jotham, Ahaz and Hezekiah, kings of Judah" (Is 1:1). If we were to spend some time mining the history of these kingships, we would learn that these royal names signal a time in Judah's history when a time of relative peace was giving way to political and military threats from nearby Assyria, which was reasserting its power after a period of slumber. Extrapolating the historical detail of Isaiah, though, is a task for another book. The point informing our purposes is that Isaiah names his time, names who he is, and names his placement within the times. Nothing of his prophecy will float above the daily realities of Judah in the days of decline. He is not interested in timeless theological proclamations as much as he is prepared to say something about the way the everlasting God will act in this situation, among these people.

Isaiah is no generic theologian, then. How could anyone be? Here is "the son of Amoz," an awfully particular means of identification, one that

lodges Isaiah right there among a family history with all of the strange
and unique specificity that comes from being in a family. The point here
is that Isaiah is not dismissing his family history for the sake of doing
some kind of "pure" theology. The words he will speak will take on a
richness of meaning precisely because he owns his deep connection to
this people in *this* time.

BEING UNDONE IN REAL PLACES

Methodologically, it is good news that theologians do not need to dis-
connect their family history from the work they do as theologians. Theologians can make great contributions when they work from particular
situations, offering those who interact with their words a type of window
into the operation of God. The faces of my friends spring to mind at this
point, the faces of theologians who have taught me and opened windows
of discovery and insight for me as they brought themselves, their history,
and their situation in life to the joyful task of theology. These are the
theologians whose work is testimony, those who speak as witnesses to
the action of an everlasting God amid their finite situations.

Of course, there is also a reserve here, methodologically. Do we not
run the risk here of collapsing God with our own experience? Is it not
possible that our own situatedness overwhelms the realities we are attempting to describe? Or, to put a finer point on it, could the God we are
attempting to describe eventually become little more than a projection
of our own experience, our hopes, or our whims?

Isaiah is remarkable at this point. There is no hint that his word-work
of prophetic truth telling is disconnected from his own place and time,
and yet there is not a moment in which Isaiah is not aware that his role
is to speak the word of the Lord. Theologians often find themselves
wedged between two approaches: either become consumed with speaking
a truth that is so all-encompassing that it has trouble responding to real
situations, or make theology primarily about "speaking my truth." Isaiah's striking approach is not interested in eternal truths that can never
touch down in the midst of a city headed for trouble. At the same time,

the truth he speaks is of the everlasting God, who is working in *this* situation, in *this* city, among *these* people.

Oftentimes, theologians are called to name the way God is working amid a particular people and specific situations, and as a matter of method to pay careful attention to how those specific particularities shape the way theology is done. Theologian Willie James Jennings outlines the theological damage that can be done when the specifics of place and people are tossed aside in the theological task. Doing so was the methodological rot in the core of theological programs that distorted the actions of slave traders into works of mercy, shot through with soteriological significance. In this mode, slave traders were "saving" those they had captured in Africa and forcibly took to other continents for sale as commodities.

Like any other calamity of Western history, theology was made to act as an accomplice, and rationale was plentifully afforded. In this case, one of the foremost methodological problems was a disconnection of doctrine from *place*. With their feet off the ground and dislodged from the distinctive features of place and people, things such as the doctrine of creation and the doctrine of salvation became involved in mapping a kind of distorted scale of goodness onto biological differences in humans. When accounting for God's work of salvation becomes disconnected from real places and real people, it allows for that account to be applied in distorted ways. For those offering theological cover for the slave trade, this method meant that God's work could be compartmentalized so that entire continents were imagined as devoid of the divine presence. Once we have made that move, "Godforsaken" places and the "Godforsaken" people who live there become objects of pity, or worse.

Ignoring the specifics of a land and a people, Jennings argues, has introduced a kind of theological method that does not allow us to see how God is working in a particular place as much as impose a vision of God's operations onto a place. "This is nothing less than a theological operation," he writes. "Like the designations of sinner and saint, convert and heretic, believer and unbeliever, faithful and apostate, this linguistic deployment alters reality, blowing by and through the specifics of identity bound to land, space, and place and narrating a new world that binds bodies to unrelenting aesthetic judgments."[2]

To sit with Isaiah, to glean from his wisdom, and to learn from the way he learned to speak in response to God is also to learn that theology is done in the midst of a people. It is to remember the way God has acted before and to recognize a divine pattern of action that is difficult to see among a people who may not be attuned to God's activity. Sometimes this means looking squarely at a situation in which a people is subjected to injustice and voicing a necessary lament. Sometimes it means helping a people to see the way they themselves have become caught up in perpetuating injustice and calling for repentance. Perhaps what makes Isaiah so effective at both is his conviction that he is not speaking anything other than a word that is faithful to God. This is not Isaiah's own truth but God's true word, which rings truly for the sake of *this* people in *this* situation. Were it anything else, Isaiah would risk presenting to the people some kind of lofty ideas or his own experience as nothing more than an idol.

UNDONE: THE LIFE OF A MODERN MARTYR

In 1930 a young theologian and pastor named Dietrich Bonhoeffer began to receive concerning reports from his native Germany while he was living and studying in New York. The academic communities that were home to his family were beginning to be shaken by an emerging antisemitism. The church communities in his native land also were not immune. The threatening thunderheads of a political storm gathered over Germany as Bonhoeffer watched from the relative isolation of New York, where he had come to study. As young Bonhoeffer considered his future, places such as Mexico and India came to mind—far away from the place where he would likely be thrust into the position of speaking into the gathering storm. The gravity of Bonhoeffer's situation confronted him

---

[2]Willie James Jennings, *The Christian Imagination: Theology and the Origins of Race* (New Haven, CT: Yale University Press, 2010), 31.

with every letter from home; if he were to return, he would be facing an inevitable confrontation between rising nationalism and the gospel he had given his life to learning and proclaiming.

Ultimately, Bonhoeffer opted to return to Germany, and there he suffered through a season of national darkness previously unimaginable. As the Nazi Party came into power, Bonhoeffer was clear-eyed about the difference between the prevailing political realities and the gospel of Jesus Christ. He was aware of the "unclean lips" that were promoting messages of biological purity and racial supremacy. Among a national church that was falling under the political persuasion of the Nazi regime, Bonhoeffer continued to adhere to the gospel, becoming more aware of the cost of being a Christian. Undoubtedly, his situation was complex, and he experienced the pressures associated with living in a world where toxic ideas were becoming commonplace. Yet, Bonhoeffer refused to extract himself from his people. As he understood it, his calling was to proclaim the gospel truthfully. His sharp theological mind produced lectures and sermons that assisted the formation of the Confessing Church, a movement that opposed Hitler's installation as the head of the church in Germany.

A 1939 invitation to New York gave Bonhoeffer a final opportunity to extract himself from the trouble his country was experiencing. His trip lasted only two weeks before he decided he needed to reverse course and head back into the storm. "I have come to the conclusion that I made a mistake in coming to America," he wrote. "I must live through this difficult period in our national history with the people of Germany." On April 9, 1945, Bonhoeffer was executed after a sham trial with no witnesses. His many acts of resistance against the regime in a time of unspeakable challenge are an enduring witness to the theological virtue of speaking the gospel in the midst of very real situations among a particular people.

The virtue of Bonhoeffer's theological life was not only in that he embodied Isaiah's prophetic work of proclamation among a people struggling to be faithful. It was also that Bonhoeffer was undone. In a 1936 letter, Bonhoeffer recounts to a friend his journey toward being undone. His story is one of having earned multiple degrees in theology while not yet having been undone by the object of theology. "I plunged into the work in a very unchristian way," he writes. "An . . . ambition that many noticed in me made my life difficult. . . . Then something happened, something that changed and transformed my life to the present day. For the first time I discovered the Bible. . . . I had often preached, I had seen a great deal of church, spoken and preached about it—but I had not yet become a Christian." It was his encounter with Jesus' Sermon on the Mount that became a turning point for Bonhoeffer, a revolutionary encounter that moved his faith from one of knowing about the kingdom Jesus was establishing to being caught up within it. "Since then everything has changed. I have felt this plainly, and so have other people about me. It was a great liberation."[3]

Being undone by this encounter made Bonhoeffer the theologian he was. In the transformation of who he was, his approach to theology changed, especially regarding doctrine. "I know that at that time [before his turning point] I turned the doctrine of Jesus Christ into something of a personal advantage for myself. . . . I pray to God that will never happen again."[4] From that point forward, Bonhoeffer's approach to theology, and to *Christology* in particular—the study of the person of Jesus Christ—took him in a different direction. He approached theology differently because he had been undone, and it allowed him to make substantial contributions, aiding the faithfulness of his people.

Today Bonhoeffer is widely considered a modern martyr. His likeness is enshrined above the doors of Westminster Abbey in London, flanked by nine other Christians from across the world who gave the last full measure of faithfulness during the twentieth century, an enduring testimony to the virtue of being undone by an encounter with God.

---

[3]Quoted in Eberhard Bethge, *Dietrich Bonhoeffer: A Biography* (Minneapolis, MN: Fortress, 2000), 204-5.
[4]Bethge, *Dietrich Bonhoeffer*, 205.

PRAYER

Holy God of love,

We thank you that you have not left us as we are.

Your life inspires us to be remade, and we ask that you meet us
in that desire.

For the times and places that we have mistaken an idol
for your holy presence,

We ask that you would restore and renew us. Remind us
of the abundance of life we find in you.

Tune our hearts, we ask, to serve the people with whom
you have placed us.

Give us a vision of the way your gospel is renewing them.

Give us eyes to see the way that you are already at work in the places
we live and serve.

Give us cause to rejoice at what you are doing.

For the sake of the redemption of the world and the glory of your name,

Shake us from all commitments that are not to you and restore us
to be your people.

Purge our lips, that we might speak your goodness.

Send us to proclaim your goodness, because you have met us through
your Spirit and Son.

Amen.

QUESTIONS FOR DISCUSSION OR REFLECTION

1. Can you relate to Isaiah's or Bonhoeffer's experiences of being undone in the awareness of your community's unfaithfulness and God's holiness? If so, how has it shaped your theological voice? If not, how will you open yourself to this experience?

2. Where have you seen theology that does not take seriously one's situation among an unfaithful people, and where have you seen theology that does? What do you see as the outcome of each? How has each kind of theology affected you?

3. Consider the historical, social, and theological realities that create your particular context. What sources for theological reflection might speak into the midst of the contextual situation you have just identified? How might you see God's work in *this* situation?

CHAPTER SEVEN

Mary

ON PONDERING

BETWEEN SINGING AND SILENCE, there is Mary. Her encounter with the divine moves her to song before it stuns her to silence. This is an enduring and unassuming declaration to those who would dare to live a God-bearing life that sometimes our best response can be one of treasuring the fleetingly thin moments when the holy pierces the overwhelming injustices of life in a fallen world.

When we meet her in the opening verses of Luke's Gospel, she is a young woman with a protest song on her lips, lyrically proclaiming praise for the God who is turning the world upside down. Hers is a song of revolution, a bold dissent in the face the mighty. "He has brought down the rulers from their thrones," she sings, "but has lifted up the humble" (Lk 1:52). And is this not exactly the kind of person we would expect to make a theological mark on the world? Is it not always the firebrand whose words reverberate most loudly? The theological contributions we often remember and celebrate most have an in-your-face, disruptive quality, and rightfully so. Let us not pretend that God's activity is not disruptive, because it is, and so the history of theology we are often given is charted according to historical hornets' nests euphemized as "turning points." Theological legacies are often forged in the fires of disruption. We remember Martin Luther with a hammer in his hand at the door of the cathedral and Dorothy Day in handcuffs on her way to jail after protesting at the White House.

Maybe these memories would be enough to sustain or encourage walking the theological life. We could turn the page on Luke's Gospel and charge ahead to Jesus' own disruption of the status quo when he picks up Isaiah's scroll and infuriates the population of his hometown (Lk 4:16-30). But that would be to forget Mary. It would be to overlook the revolutionary silence that is just as loud as her song. It would be to forsake an essential quality of the work of theology that she refuses to abandon: pondering.

That is why I love that we find Mary *between* singing and silence. She is not entirely silent, and she also has the courage to ponder. Undoubtedly, there are times and spaces where the beautiful simplicity of stillness and the serenity of pondering are part of walking the theological life, and we will learn more about this from Mary shortly. At the same time, I am immediately disquieted by the reminder that Mary's life is often portrayed in an almost mythical repose. Sometimes, Mary's "let it be unto me" posture toward God has mutated into a popular caricature of a docile—almost wistful—young mother who cares for Jesus, unaffected by the world around her. If we are not careful, we may think we have found a Disney princess in the opening chapters of Luke. Mary's silent mystique is reinforced every December as we sing Christmas carols about silent, peaceful nights and a newborn baby who somehow did not cry.

But Mary's world was not silent, and I am quite sure that the baby cried. Jesus was born right into the middle of trouble. I am still not sure how to reconcile the lyric "all is calm, all is bright" with the reality of Herod's soldiers hunting for Jesus with orders to kill in hand. This is precisely why we need a reminder that Mary's pondering—even in silence—was a revolutionary virtue. It was part of her troubled world being turned upside down by the goodness of God. For those of us peering over Luke's shoulder at Mary's life in hopes that she will teach us a little something about how we might do theology, we will find not only that pondering has social and political ramifications but also that it allows some of our closely held beliefs about God to be challenged, renewed, and reimagined. Pondering may be quiet, but it summons revolution. It is the space where Mary connects God's activity to the realities of the troubled world. Her pondering is a generous theological arena where she does not shut down or put away the possibility that she is holding God in her arms merely because God has not acted like that before. Presented with something utterly and completely new, she postures for receptivity and connection.

Inviting Mary's instruction on pondering and silence allows her to teach us to respond to the divine by walking a God-bearing life in the world. Hers is a surprising lesson, especially for those of us who are prone to make our own words the focus of our theological work. While we fixate on how to use the right words to describe the divine life, or even how to maximize the impact of our words in praise to the God who is making all things new, Mary reminds us that at least part of our work is pondering and treasuring God's activity without uttering a syllable.

Additionally, Mary is the living critique of the modern temptation to separate theology from spirituality. Her life tends to blur whatever lines we modern people have drawn between the two. At once she is responding to God's activity in words—the work of theology!—and issuing an invitation for us to join her in silent, transformative astonishment at what we have seen. For those walking the pathway of the theological life, she beckons us into a way that includes silence, wonder, and astonishment. "Our theology can become corrupted because we neglect to attend to our lives," Kelly Kapic wisely reminds us, "for true theology must always be true spirituality."[1] The theological life happens between silence and praise. It is there we find Mary, a good and virtuous partner along the way.

THE SILENCE OF PRAISE

The way Luke tells it, the events surrounding Jesus' birth made for a busy time around Bethlehem. For a few days, that sleepy little agricultural settlement became the center of attention and activity, both human and

---

[1]Kelly Kapic, *A Little Book for New Theologians: Why and How to Study Theology* (Downers Grove, IL: IVP Academic, 2012), 45.

divine. In Luke's account, a familiar pattern begins to emerge. It is the give-and-take of proclamation and pondering, commendation and quiet, movement and stillness.

Table 7.1. Action and Contemplation in the Infancy Narrative in Luke

Lk 2:14	"Glory to God in the highest heaven"	"and on earth *peace* . . ."
Lk 2:16	So [the shepherds] *hurried off* and found Mary and Joseph, and the baby	who was *lying* in the manger.
Lk 2:17-19	When they had seen him, they *spread the word*	But Mary treasured up all these things and *pondered* them in her heart.

Among the hurried and busy work of proclaiming theological discovery, of extolling the God who is turning the world upside down, the theme of pondering provides an interruption to the intense current of action words surrounding the birth of the Messiah. Mary's pondering is an oasis of calm in a sandstorm of activity. In a sentence about her pondering, Luke creates room for us to stop, breathe, and join Mary in her pondering. This is all well and good, but what does this have to do with the work of theology?

Pondering, at least for Luke, is no idle or empty wondering. Pondering is not mindlessness. It is active and dynamic. In fact, when Luke describes Mary's pondering, he chooses a word that signals things or people coming together to meet or confer.[2] We could think of pondering as an arena, opening a space for things that might be distant or unrelated to come together in surprising and refreshing ways. In Mary's pondering, an array of theological revelation is opening: the meeting together of God and flesh, the injustices of life colliding with the righteousness of God, and in what may be a foreshadowing of Acts, the coming together of Jews and Gentiles in a new community that no one could have imagined—except, perhaps, Mary.

I sometimes think of Mary when I am working with a theology student who comes to a new understanding of the way God is at work

---

[2]The Greek term *sym ballō* occurs in Lk 2:19; 14:31; Acts 4:15; 17:18; 18:27; 20:14. Some translations place "ponder" in Lk 1:29, but the Greek word is different there, so "wondering" or "reasoning" may be a better translation choice in that case.

in the world. On some days, it happens in a private conversation or during a lecture when I hear them utter something like, "Whoa . . ." I can tell that the arena is open, and some dynamic theological work is taking place. Like Mary's pondering, theirs may very well be the space that allows the meeting of real-world issues and divine activity, the meeting of closely held notions about God and God's actual action, the meeting of expectations and hopes with divine nearness, the meeting of different things we have seen previously that make sense in light of what God is doing. In the space opened by pondering, new depths of understanding begin to emerge.

These are the students who have held space and held their tongues, at least long enough to give themselves over to pondering. Again, Mary's virtue speaks: not all theological work is about the words we produce. Often, theological work is about giving ourselves the time and space to allow a meeting together of ideas and possibilities.

In a phrase, pondering is the work of a theologian in developing *imagination*. Of course, I do not mean something like "make-believe" when I use that term. Rather, it is something closer to the astonishment a very young woman might experience when she holds a baby in her arms whom she is having trouble believing she bore and who also happens to be God in the flesh. Pondering opens the room to imagine what could be possible with God in her arms. Pondering allows the meeting together of the very real situations Mary faces in her everyday life with the present nearness of the divine.

This is the kind of imagination theologians develop to do the work of "thinking what to say to be saying the gospel."[3] In other words, without a theological imagination that allows us to see the meeting together of divine action with our created world, we probably are not doing the work of theology. Part of the theological life is developing the capacity to see the surprising work of God *as the work of God*. It is the kind of imagination that allowed Mary to see an unexpected pregnancy as the work of

---

[3]Robert Jenson, *Systematic Theology*, vol. 1, *The Triune God* (Oxford: Oxford University Press, 1997), 32.

God, so much so that she could understand it as part of what God was doing to bring salvation to the world.

Beyond an agenda to be open-minded, this is a theological virtue dating back thousands of years. Many of the early ecumenical councils—meetings of Christians throughout the first centuries of the church's life to determine matters of doctrine—were not only places of debate but places of pondering. The theologians who comprised the delegations to those councils were courageous enough to ponder new connections about God and God's activity in the world. They were, of course, working out matters of how the activity they saw in Jesus was consistent with what our Israelite ancestors had seen in God, but they also did not shy away from the possibility that God's activity had been extended in an unexpected and disruptive way.

Theology has the delightful task of pointing to a thing God does and identifying it as God's activity, especially when it is offbeat, disruptive, or unexpected. We do this by giving the story of Scripture a position of authority in our communities, reminding ourselves of the kinds of patterns we have seen before, and asking whether what we think we see God doing now is consistent with what we have seen God do before.

There are several contemporary approaches to theology—sometimes we call them theological methods—that are known for this. Various forms of *liberation theology*, a method in which theology is done by asking about God's activity in freeing human beings from oppression or violence, tend to lead with a reading of Exodus. If God was freeing the covenant people of Israel from captivity and oppression then, does that not give us a vision of how God is continuing to unshackle people today? *Feminist theology* is known for a similar method. Its approach is to remind the church that God's activity in the world has always included women and calls the contemporary church to align its practices with what we have seen God do in not just Mary's life, but also the lives of such women as Junia (Rom 16:7), and Priscilla (Acts 18:26; Rom 16:3; 1 Cor 16:19).

In that sense, theology is not exactly a creative endeavor because theologians are not inventing new things. Rather, theology is a constructive venture, a practice of seeing and describing the way God's work is continuing to weave a new reality in the world. Theologians such as James Cone draw attention to the connection between Jesus' crucifixion and the real-life nightmare of Black people being lynched. Jeremy Begbie, another contemporary theologian, helps articulate the way the realities of God's creative work can be known in music and the arts. A host of other theologians are exploring the way God's activity is redemptively present in science, pop culture, psychology, economics, and the list goes on. That is the kind of work that calls for the development of theological imagination. That is the kind of work that calls for pondering.

This is why pondering is no passive lack of engagement. Guided by Mary's example, our pondering is a virtuous act of wonder, an active fullness evoked by what we see in the activity of God. "Theology is necessarily the logic of wonders," Karl Barth helpfully reminds us. Beyond a pattern of ideas, the theo-logic of wonder is the astonishment induced by God's remaking the world, turning it upside down. It is the strange logic that arouses Mary to sing and to ponder, all because of the event of God's entrance into the world through her womb as the infant Jesus. "He is the miracle, the miracle of all miracles!" says Barth. "Christ is that infinitely wondrous event which compels a person . . . to be necessarily, profoundly, wholly and irrevocably, astonished."[4]

Granted, Mary's pondering may not be synonymous with astonishment, at least in the way Barth proposes it in the life of the theologian. Still, Mary's witness is teaching us that one of the ways we can respond to God is to set speaking aside for a time and to simply ponder the goodness of what is happening in front of our eyes. There will always be a tug on the theologian to speak. But giving space to see God's activity meeting the world's deep need is also a necessary skill. For the life of a theologian, the inward is not to be neglected in favor of the outward life of publishing and publicity. While theologians are rightly moved to praise through words, we are also rightfully stilled to silence.

---

[4]Karl Barth, *Evangelical Theology: An Introduction* (Grand Rapids, MI: Eerdmans, 1963), 66, 71.

IN PRAISE OF SILENCE

The theological life is often characterized by what one says. Theological careers can be measured by publications, presentations, sermons, or social media shares. Theological *lives*, on the other hand, will need to make room for pondering and some silence. Following Mary's lead, silence too can be a response to the work of the divine, revealing more than it is concealing.

Silence has long been recognized as a vital spiritual practice. It has "worked like an underground stream down the centuries, penetrating and nourishing the Church far more deeply and widely than its usual hiddenness might suggest."[5] At the same time, silence can also be a stream of theological wisdom, a methodological partner to speech, opening the space we need to evaluate what has been spoken. In Mary's life, virtue is found in the way her description of God's activity and the spiritual practice of silence cannot be separated from each other, as can be the case in the way theology is often done. Mary holds these together, reminding us that the theological life is at once about praising God in words and holding space to not speak.

The work of a theologian, whether pastoral or academic, is often plagued with the pressure to say the next thing. There are sermons to write, lectures to prepare, articles to publish, inspiring words to be shared at the next church event, or the next social media post to formulate. Amid that tension, silence stills us, opening a place for pondering without pressuring us to say anything. While pastoral theology often takes place in never-ending loop of counting down to Sunday, and academic theology tends to be compelled by the demand to produce papers, presentations, and lectures, silence is the companion who reminds us that not all theology takes place in what we are producing. Without applying demands to make our observations into something that others can consume, admire, or critique, silence calls us to wonder and delight, to be enchanted by God without ever asking us to produce a thing.

---

[5]David F. Ford and Daniel W. Hardy, *Living in Praise: Worshipping and Knowing God* (Grand Rapids, MI: Baker Academic, 2005), 27.

Recognizing the virtue of silence in the work of theology, a host of the ancients pointed toward a method of doing theology we now call *apophatic theology*. Arguing that the absolute transcendence of God places God far above what human knowledge can attain or words can describe, theologians such as Gregory of Nyssa, Basil the Great, and John Chrysostom suggested that we actually come to know God in what we cannot say rather than in what we can say. Apophatic theology, then, walks with a humble posture, always aware that the moment we say something about God, it will by definition fall inadequate at some point. Perhaps, this method suggests, it would be right and good for us to fall silent in the presence of the divine. Silence is the surrender into the mystery.

Such surrender became a matter of playful debate when a theology professor friend once shared an image of a fill-in-the-blank test from a college theology course she was teaching. When a student was asked to define apophatic theology, the answer space was left blank, and no one could determine whether this was due to forgetfulness or next-level brilliance. As I recall, the student received credit for the silent answer.

Apophatic, or negative theology, as it is sometimes called, opens a space for silence in recognition that words cannot fill the place God occupies. God's existence is not existence as such, apophatic reasoning contends, precisely because as the uncreated Creator, God does not exist as we do, being dependent on another for existence. To be sure, apophatic method is a helpful friend to theologians who have come to trust in our ability to neatly define how God lives and moves, blowing open the categories and allowing holy mystery to enliven our theological imagination. It is to remind us of the luminous darkness that is God and to forge a place of encounter, as St. John of the Cross has it, that "darkens the mind . . . only to give it light in everything."[6]

There is freedom in silence for the theologian because silence is not mere lack or emptiness, at least not for the work of theology. In the

---

[6]St. John of the Cross, *The Dark Night of the Soul* (London: Thomas Baker, 1916), 108.

theological life, silence is a place of abundance and extravagance. It is the space in which we can respond to the overwhelming goodness of the divine without having to produce words at all. It is the place where we can treasure what we have witnessed in the work of God, where we are given permission to not spin out our latest discovery into a sermon, lecture, or blog post. We are given the blessing of simply delighting in the goodness of God.

Silence also opens a place for us to make synthetic connections we may not have seen before. Silence may be quiet, but it is not always inactive. Often, taking time to be quiet and simply ponder the goodness of God creates a space of meeting, where we can not only meet with the goodness of God but also allow new points of theological connection to find one another. In locating herself between praise and silence, incorporating both into her response to God's address, Mary finds herself as a faithful observer of God's activity in the world. For her and for us, silence is not an emptiness but a fullness.

SILENCE AND THE SONG OF REVOLUTION

Sometimes the work of theology involves singing songs of praise to God for the revolution that has taken place in Jesus Christ. N. T. Wright, reminding us yet again that the first-century followers of Jesus had a quite different understanding of faith than we late moderns do, speaks plainly of what they saw as they watched Jesus die on the cross: "They saw it as the day the revolution began. . . . They were talking about something bigger, something more dangerous, something altogether more explosive" than a faith that was exclusively what happens to us spiritually after we die.[7]

While I think Wright offers a vivid and fruitful assessment of the way Jesus' original followers saw his ministry, I happen to think that Mary saw the revolution beginning around his birth just as much as in his death and crucifixion. Either way, Mary steps forth in the literature of the

---

[7]N. T. Wright, *The Day the Revolution Began: Reconsidering the Meaning of Jesus's Crucifixion* (San Francisco: HarperOne, 2016), 4.

New Testament as a soloist who falls silent, disclosing a glimpse of the apocalyptic choir that would join her in Revelation. While the book of Revelation is often noted for the visual images it evokes (horsemen, battles, beasts, and the like), it is also rich in the way it calls us to hear sound and sit in silence. To read Revelation is to be treated to a symphony of praise punctuated by arresting silence. Juxtaposed with booming peals of thunder and the sounding of trumpets are times of silence, where all is stilled (Rev 8:1-13). Ryan Hansen's insightful work on this acoustic association points toward silence and praise as the soundtrack of revolution for early Christians.[8] "God's activity is described in terms of unmaking and making new the entire universe," he writes. That making and remaking can be seen in the movement between vocalizing praise and holding space for silence. "On the other side of the saints' vocation of silence, which negates the Roman world," Hansen says, "is their work of praise, which enables them to participate in the new heavens and new earth."[9]

Perhaps Mary is a prototypical member of Revelation's saintly choir. Between singing and silence, she is a firsthand witness to the powers and principalities being subverted by God's humble entrance into our world. She can sing of God's action in overturning the old creation and ponder in silent awe the way that God is opening the new.

Of course, political alignments, military powers, and economic forces were just as much in play in Mary's world as they are in ours, and so when she receives word that God has charted a course into the world through her own body in a forgotten corner of Galilee, one might expect her to throw her hat in the ring and join the fray. It could be that her newfound position would finally give her a voice of influence among her people or the foreign military force that was governing her people at the time. But Mary sings of God's activity and then, anticipating the words of a

---

[8]For a fascinating extrapolation of silence and singing in Revelation, see Ryan Leif Hansen, *Silence and Praise: Rhetorical Cosmology and Political Theology in the Book of Revelation* (Minneapolis, MN: Fortress, 2014).

[9]Hansen, *Silence and Praise*, 153-55.

yet-to-be-written song of praise, begins to "ponder anew what the Almighty can do."[10]

This, I suspect, carries a common temptation for theologians. In a world where the loudest voices seem to set the categories and the agendas, there will likely be a stirring among those who care about the world to use our voices, as we rightly should. It is at this point that theologians need to remember to use their voices *as theologians*. Our work is distinctive, powerful work. Learning from Mary, we are reminded that theology involves using our voices to proclaim God's distinctive revolution that is happening in Jesus Christ. It is also to ponder in awe and then to sing again. Our work is not to make the world as we would have it but to notice and proclaim what God is already doing to make all things new.

This is the kind of thing that will often call us to silence. Pondering in silence will allow us to center God's activity rather than our own. It opens the space for us to be theologians, precisely because the thing we will say flows from what we are seeing in the activity of God. This is what distinguishes theologians from other activists and social workers; our work is the overflow from the arena where we have seen God's distinctive work intersect the world's deepest needs. Being able to see that and then to sing will often require silence. "In silence," Ruth Hailey Barton wisely counsels, "there is the potential for each of us to 'know that I am God' with such certainty that the competing powers of evil and sin and the ego-self can no longer hold us in their grasp."[11]

Between silence and praise, Mary's life is the soundtrack to a theological life well lived. In her we find embodied the virtue of being open to being confronted with God's surprising activity in Jesus Christ. Mary does not just accept it. She treasures it. Yes, the theological life includes stillness and pondering, and it may be in just those places that we come

---

[10]Joachim Neander, "Praise to the Lord, the Almighty," trans., Catherine Winkworth, in *Sing to the Lord* (Kansas City, MO: Lillenas, 1993), 20.

[11]Ruth Hailey Barton, *Invitation to Solitude and Silence: Experiencing God's Transforming Presence* (Downers Grove, IL: InterVarsity Press, 2010), 31.

face to face with our most significant challenges. Cherished beliefs may be called into question. Possibilities we had not yet considered stretch our understanding. Old loyalties may need to be surrendered. It can all be so uncomfortable that we may be tempted to turn away from the theological life altogether.

Still, Mary is a good companion on the journey, reminding us to open space to ponder. Pondering is always for the sake of increased faithfulness to God. Pondering does not throw out the old merely because it falls out of fashion, but gives us the space to connect notions in ways that deepen and expand our knowledge of God.

PONDERING IN TEXAS

"I don't know what to do with what I experienced," a theology student once said to me. "I'm not sure how to explain to people what it was that I encountered this summer and how it changed me." It was one of those after-class conversations where the content of the lecture and a difficult, disruptive experience fuse into the moments that theological educators live for. "I mean, I've been sitting here throughout this class session wanting to say something because the lecture's giving words to what I saw and experienced, but every time I thought I might say something, I felt like my words weren't going to do justice to God's work I saw."

The work this young theologian witnessed was among the three thousand people of an often-forgotten migrant town on the dusty plains of Texas. Offering a couple of months of service there, especially to the children of the town, had given her a new capacity to see the odd mystery of God's holy work. She had taken yet another step down the bafflingly beautiful pathway of a theological life, and the heartache evoked by her encounter with hardship and the holiness of God were swirling together. Surprisingly, she encountered holiness, far, far away from the stained glass and vaulted ceilings of the church that had nurtured her. "How do I even describe this?" she asked.

I had no answer for her. There was no set of steps I could offer that would give her precisely what she was hoping for. I had, however, recently been reading about another young woman who pondered things she could not explain, and so I responded, "I'm not sure. But you remind me of Mary."

In those moments, this student was walking in Mary's example, following her in creating a space that was not flooded with words. It was a pondering space where the trouble of the world could be seen anew in light of God's entrance into it. Mary's method of silence and pondering became a legitimating way of walking the theological life for a young theologian beginning her journey.

Sometimes the response of theologians is not to speak but to ponder the goodness of God's work in our hearts. It is to sit in wonder of the beautifully strange reality that is being born into the world in unexpected places. Even while the rest of the world hurriedly goes about churning out the words of proclamation as publicly as possible, we can, alongside Mary, hold an active silence of wonder. We can open our hearts to facilitate the meeting of divine mystery and worldly reality, and even if it does not produce a word, we can know, with Mary, that we are still walking the theological life.

PRAYER

God of revolutionary redemption,
My soul glorifies you;
My spirit rejoices in God my Savior.
I am your servant; may it be to me according to your word.
Grant that I may be able to see the way you are making the world new.
Grant that I may be able to treasure what you are giving.
May I be faithful to bear the good news of the world's redemption,
To be a vessel where silence and praise meet,
That your mercy may be enacted in the world through your servant.
Amen.

QUESTIONS FOR DISCUSSION OR REFLECTION

1. In what ways are you tempted to separate theology from spirituality? How might Mary's life offer instruction on bringing the two together in your own life?

2. In what ways do you think you could become more of an arena where God's work and the world's need meet? How can you create space for silence and pondering in your days, starting now?

3. How do you understand God's activity of revolution in your work as a theologian? Have you ever seen or felt the effects of revolutionary theology proclaimed *without* a practice of silence? How will you incorporate silence in personally understanding and publicly communicating God's revolution?

CHAPTER EIGHT

John the Baptist

ON STANDING AT THE EDGE

WHAT DO YOU SAY ABOUT YOURSELF?

John the Baptist has the distinction of being the first figure in the Gospel accounts, and it is there that we will begin exploring. Mark's Gospel, having been written first among the four, opens with John the Baptist appearing in the wilderness and baptizing people in the Jordan River (Mk 1:1-8). The other three Gospel writers include John in their accounts, of course, with Luke situating the birth and ministry of this eccentric figure toward the beginning of his account as well. In fact, placing John's ministry at the beginning of their accounts may be one of the most common links among all four Gospel accounts. Even as John's Gospel departs the Synoptic pattern of announcing Jesus, it still includes a prophetic figure out on the edge of the wilderness, proclaiming that someone else will follow him, "the straps of whose sandals I am not worthy to untie" (Jn 1:27). Placing John the Baptist up front is not simply an honor of who got to be first; there is, rather, significance in John's announcing who will come after him. By placing John right up front, we can see the virtues of one who announces the gospel.

Of course, not all theologians are called to the same kind of ministry John the Baptist had. We need to be clear that in the body of Christ, there is a diversity of calling, and we need Mary's calling just as much as we need John's, for example. There is, though, a virtue that all four Gospel writers seem to want to uphold around John, and that is his insistence that he points to Jesus. While he announces the good news of the gospel, he also points away from himself. "He did not fail to confess," we read in John 1, "but confessed freely, 'I am not the Messiah'" (Jn 1:20).

This free confession follows the developing interest in John that seems to mount over time. "Who are you?" the priests ask, having sought him out. "Give us an answer to take back to those who sent us. What do you say about yourself?" (Jn 1:22). As much as we tend to evaluate theologians by what they say about God, there is wisdom in asking what we say about ourselves. To put a finer point on it, who do you consider yourself to be as a theologian, especially in relationship to the message you proclaim?

WHAT DO WE SAY OF OURSELVES?

The community that nurtured me held a revered place for theologians, even if theology itself was sometimes viewed as being too impractical to do any good. Across the years, it has been interesting to listen in on what is said about theologians. "I never really understood everything he said," a retired pastor friend of mine said about a longtime theology professor who taught him, "but he was just so smart. He still impresses me." This is a sentiment, I suspect, that lives on in many church traditions. Theologians can be viewed as inscrutable gurus, the ones who speak in the tongues of angels or, perhaps, sanctified know-it-alls. Rarely do I hear the same mythology grow around other forms of ministry, and there can be a bit of a vocational danger in setting theologians up as those who exist on a different spiritual plane because we have been called to study the things of God.

If we shift the context, we might find that the things others say about theologians alter dramatically. Outside church circles, people can be confused about what a theologian does or what theology is at all. Some of my favorite moments of cultural reorientation tend to happen when I am at or traveling to a conference or gathering of theologians. Sometimes, a "senior scholar," as we will often say—academic parlance for a well-known theologian—will be pressed into a situation that calls for them to try to explain what they do to someone who does not know who they are. While they may have just delivered a groundbreaking paper that promises to rewrite the field for a generation, the man on the bus sitting next to them after the lecture is simply trying to understand why anyone would travel to listen to someone talk about God for an hour or more.

Sometimes it can be even more combative. When I tell people I am a theologian, I know I must be prepared for any number of responses, from the perplexed to the frustrated. "It's a waste of time," some people might say, going on to challenge me on some point of theology or even the validity of theology itself.

Overall, in a world where people are saying lots of different things about theologians, it is important to ask what we say of ourselves. Developing language around our vocation is a vital part of developing the virtues of the theological life. I once listened to a lecture in which a theologian used a set of hand gestures to signify the place of his vocation. "Not only am I ordained," he said, holding one hand horizontally in front of his face, "but I'm a theologian." His other hand moved into place, hovering about six inches above the other, signifying that his vocation was somehow above that of laypersons, pastors, and others who were ordained to "lesser" roles. That image still sits uneasily in my memory.

Perhaps, then, this is why I am drawn to John the Baptist's words about himself and how they offer to us a virtuous example of how we speak about ourselves. "I am the voice of one calling in the wilderness," he says, "'Make straight the way for the Lord'" (Jn 1:23). In every account we have of John's responses, especially when others are interested in what he has to say, he points away from himself. He is, as he says it, the voice of one calling. What remains clear about John's understanding of his vocation is that he is not the anointed one and that his ministry is to call out in preparation for the one who is to come.

To be sure, this does not mean that John's voice goes silent. No one who shrinks back from a vocation to call out powerful and well-intentioned religious people says the kinds of things John the Baptist does to that "brood of vipers" who make their way out to be baptized by him (Mt 3:7). John's words are prophetically pointy, but he uses them only in preparation for the Lord's nearness. The virtue of the theological life we find in him, then, is the capacity to speak clearly and potently, even while what he says about himself remains vocationally clear. His job is to prepare the way for the Lord. It is to announce that a radical change in the world is at hand, enacted not by him but by the one who will baptize with the Spirit. John is, like the calling of a theologian, seeking to say what must be said to announce the gospel, powerfully and potently. At the same time, the message he announces does not seek to remake the world as he would have it be. The things John says about himself stem from a clear understanding of his vocation, which is to announce God's coming into the world.

How might the vocation of a theologian respond to this kind of virtuous speaking? How might theology be done, shaped, and situated if it were to join John in preparing the way of the Lord? How might we understand our calling as theologians not as a kind of intellectual lordship over other callings, nor as a disposable and worthless whistling into the wind of a modern world? The words we are called to speak flow from a vocation that is exemplified in what John says of himself: "I'm not the Messiah, but let me tell you about the one who is."

A WITNESS TO THE LIGHT

"There was a man sent from God whose name was John. He came as a witness to testify concerning that light, so that through him all might believe. He himself was not the light; he came only as a witness to the light" (Jn 1:6-8). Granted, John the Baptist held a unique role in the way God's gospel was announced. We would go too far in claiming, for example, that theologians can step directly into John's unique shoes. There is a dynamic at play here, however, that informs the ongoing work of theology, namely that John is a witness to the light.

Immediately, this presents a fascinating portrait of a locust-eating baptizer because he is not afraid to pronounce some difficult things while also recognizing that he is not the one that will set all things in order. He is a witness to the light, but not the light itself. On this point, John's virtue confronts the temptation that lurks in the work of theology to pronounce the way things should be as if that were the offer of salvation itself. We will explore this in more detail in the section to follow, but for now, I do not want this to escape our attention. John's work is not to save the world or straighten it out. His job, rather, is to make straight the path for the one who will.

As he is presented in the Gospel accounts, John has a distinctly virtuous way of being humble about what he is not, even as he boldly proclaims what God is doing. Our ancestors in the faith, beginning with the biblical writers and continuing on with those who declared their writing to be authoritative for the Christian church, signal to us that John's example is one to be followed here. To be sure, John is more than a moralistic example or prototype of a theologian; it is the virtue we find in his life that instructs our own work of theology. His method is shaped by what the church has come to see as a virtue, which is acting as a witness to God's work rather than attempting to do the work under his own steam.

Whether our theological work is pastoral, academic, or something in between, we will likely face the temptation to do what we can to act in the world, confronting the evil that causes its groans. Acting in the world, of course, is nothing short of what God has done and continues to do, calling the church to continually act as the body of Christ. Yet, we do so reminding ourselves and others that our work is not our own. The redemption of the world is not a strategy we have devised, and the virtue we find in John's work is the humility to acknowledge that theological reality. To be sure, John was deeply engaged in the prophetic work of proclaiming and enacting God's redemption, so deeply involved that he proclaimed it through his martyrdom. Still, his fierce perseverance always acknowledged that his work was not to make the world as he would want it but to prepare for the world as God wants it.

Humility is what allows John to do theological work virtuously. Sometimes we fight to remake the world as we want it because we assume that must be the way God wants it. John's example, however, is a reminder that we are not the light, and our actions must always take that reality into account. The unquestioned assumption that our action is what God wants is a theological error that opens the door not only for moral calamity but also for a severely compromised witness. "I am not the light" may be the beginning of virtue for those called to cry out in the wilderness.

BEYOND THE JORDAN

Geography matters, especially in the way John tells stories in his Gospel. When he points out a particular location, we can be sure that it matters for the things that are happening. Among the Gospel writers, he is alone in saying that John the Baptist's ministry was taking place "beyond" or "on the other side of the Jordan" (Jn 1:28), depending on the translation.

For those who first read this Gospel, the meaning would not have been lost on them. Everything beyond the Jordan was wilderness territory. The river where John baptized was a borderland separating the blessings of the Promised Land from the desolation of the desert. Beyond mere material provision, though, going beyond the Jordan carried the risk of encountering the unsavory and bizarre kinds of forces that God kept at bay in land where milk and honey flowed. In a different geographical crossing, Mark sends chills down the spines of his original readers when he recalls, "That day when evening came, [Jesus] said to his disciples, 'Let us go over to the other side'" (Mk 4:35). We may miss the unnerving message here, but the disciples did not: you do not go to the other side of the Sea of Galilee, especially when it is dark! Of course, Jesus does, and if the storm that nearly sinks their boat is not enough to confirm their feelings, then there is their welcoming committee on the other side—a demon-possessed man who lives among the (unclean) dead bodies buried in the caves and a herd of (unclean) swine. Everything about the other side signified chaos, disorder, unclean, and unruly realities. And that is precisely where John the Baptist sets his ministry.

Three geographical realities with methodological possibility show up in John's ministry. First, he is working outside Jerusalem. Second, he is located in a border territory. Third, his ministry is situated between promise and wilderness. Looking at these three aspects, we can draw on the virtues of his work to inform our own.

Outside Jerusalem. Being outside Jerusalem is a major theme for all the Gospel writers as they discuss John. Some place more emphasis on this than others, but the simple reality is that John is doing his work outside the center of theological and political power. Often theologians refer to this as doing theology from the margins. John the Baptist is a marginal figure, one who is decentered from the cultural, religious, and intellectual capital of Jerusalem.

For those of us who have grown up far away from places like Jerusalem, it is difficult for us to understand the kind of power and centrality that was signified in Jerusalem. Not only was it where the presence of God had dwelled, but for many of its residents throughout history, it represented the navel of the world, a kind of central place that united the planet. Beyond the geographical significance, John's ancestors knew nothing of separating powers between religion and government. For generations, all political power in Jerusalem was inherently religious; the temple, where the presence of the Lord resided, was also meant to be the palace. "Within Israel," Rodney Clapp writes, "the temple bore manifold social, spiritual, political, economic and cultural importance. In Contemporary America it would be the equivalent of the entire range of our iconic political and cultural institutions: the White House, Capitol Hill, the National Cathedral, Wall Street and Hollywood."[1]

During John's lifetime, Jerusalem was occupied by Rome, but it was still nearly impossible to distinguish between religious and political power in that city. Though Jerusalem was under occupation by the Roman Empire, an arrangement allowing the Jewish people to live and worship according to their customs also meant that some alliances between Jewish and Roman authorities were going to be necessary to

---

[1]Rodney Clapp, *A Peculiar People: The Church as Culture in a Post-Christian Society* (Downers Grove, IL: InterVarsity Press, 1996), 86.

support the arrangement. A Roman military base was constructed near the temple; military force was never far from the center of religious life.

Understanding the theological virtues of John's ministry, then, calls us to recognize that his marginalization was not a liability. Indeed, it was his distance from the prevailing systems that allowed him to see the broader thing God was working in the world. "Do not begin to say to yourselves, 'We have Abraham as our father,'" he says to those who are coming out to the margins from Jerusalem. "For I tell you out of these stones God can raise up children for Abraham. The ax is already at the root of the trees, and every tree that does not produce good fruit will be cut down and thrown into the fire" (Lk 3:8-9). The message is not that having Abraham as a father is bad but that John is against creating an establishment so rooted and centered in a dominant identity that the poor can be forgotten. We remember John so vividly in the Gospels because his message from the margins offers a way of life and salvation for those who are so deeply embedded in the centers of power that they have trouble seeing a way down the path of faithfulness.

The speaking of gospel truth to power is rarely an easy vocation, but it is part of the virtue we see in the way John does his theological work. Often, speaking this kind of truth to power will leave the theologian a bit displaced from centers of social power. *Solitude* was what Karl Barth named this dynamic. For him, solitude was not in an individual theologian being alone but about the theologian coming to occupy the rhythms and logic of the theological life, which are simply different from those of the centers of power. "It is likely that theology will scarcely ever become popular," he warns, "as little with the pious as with the children of this world, precisely because of the ethical and practical disturbance that issues from it directly and indirectly."[2] The point, of course, is that the kind of work theologians do will never fit hand-in-glove into the centers of power. The gospel, by its nature, brings a redemptive disruption according to its own logic. The news it proclaims is usually not

---

[2]Karl Barth, *Evangelical Theology: An Introduction* (Grand Rapids, MI: Eerdmans, 1963), 119.

seen as good by the brokers of power, who have an interest in maintaining the old creation rather than welcoming the new.

There is a reason John the Baptist is never quoted in Dale Carnegie's bestselling *How to Win Friends and Influence People*.[3] Calling a group coming to you for baptism a brood of vipers is rarely a way to acquire a lot of popularity (Mt 3:7). We would miss the point, too, if we thought that becoming a theologian would give us a special dispensation to be outright nasty with other people. John's work is simply not going to fit the Jerusalem establishment; his proclamation of the Lord's coming will not allow him to comfortably walk to the rhythms of political and social power.

Still, we should recognize that political power itself is not an automatic enemy of theology. Theologians across history have worked diligently on the proper arrangement of political power and the claims of theology. In John's ministry, however, we see that his commitment to proclaiming God's particular arrival will not always fit the dynamics of the political and social interests of the old creation. John's focus is not on fighting political interests but on faithful proclamation of the goodness of God. His commitment to proclaiming God's activity is primary in his work; he does not seek conflict, but his faithfulness to the message of God's kingdom sometimes puts him out of step with those around him.

In a border territory. The second geographical insight has to do with John's work in a border territory. Borders have often come to signify a boundary between one territory and another, a barrier. It is interesting to note, however, that John's ministry is taking place "beyond" the Jordan. That is, he is not held back by the Jordan as a particular boundary. In proclaiming the coming of God, John's ministry has a transgressive, edgy nature that points to a type of theological virtue. He is undoubtedly seeking to be faithful to God and the message of God's entrance into the world, even as he transgresses boundaries and expectations.

This kind of virtue is manifested in several ways theologically. Sometimes theologians transgress the boundaries set between fields of study.

---

[3]Dale Carnegie, *How to Win Friends and Influence People* (New York: Simon & Schuster, 1936).

Over the past half century, academic theology has sought conversation partners with a growing number of fields, expanding the kinds of questions and issues theology explores. Theology's engagement with science tends to attract a lot of attention, though its engagement with art, philosophy, the social sciences, and many more is also making significant contributions. Taking John as an example in this kind of work, we can see that this is not a mere fusion, where the presuppositions of both fields are melded or ignored. Part of what makes John so interesting is his commitment to his own distinct message. When the Gospel writers tell us that he wore clothes made of camel's hair and grasshoppers were his main source of nutrition, we are reminded that he is not only a prophetic figure but also a *distinctive* figure, proclaiming a unique message. Theologians are under no obligations to give up the distinctive features of their field to engage in interdisciplinary work. In fact, maintaining our distinctive methods, commitments, and message offers a truly interesting way to engage in conversation with other fields.

One example of this can be seen in theology's engagement with science, though these points can apply to interdisciplinary engagements more broadly. Especially among those just beginning in the interchange, the tendency can be to try to harmonize the conversation in a way that asks theology to do some science and calls for science to do a little theology. Ian Barbour identifies six varieties of interaction between theology and science: conflict, independence, dialogue, integration, consonance, and assimilation.[4] In reflecting on these, John Polkinghorne offers this vital methodological observation: "Just as the object of scientific enquiry is the physical world, so the object of theological enquiry is God."[5] This is not to say that one cannot address the other, because Polkinghorne finds dialogue and integration to be the two most promising modes of theology and science interacting with each other. Holding theology *as* theology and science *as* science allows a robust

[4]Cited in John Polkinghorne, *Science and Theology: An Introduction* (Minneapolis, MN: Fortress, 1998), 20-22.
[5]Polkinghorne, *Science and Theology*, 20.

conversation to unfold, so that one does not collapse into the other or call the other to operate according to the one's methods and commitments. If theology attempts to understand God through the methods of science, for example, God becomes another physical or natural reality to be studied, just more of the same but in a religious mode. "In the case of science," Polkinghorne continues,

> the dimension of reality concerned is that of a physical world that we transcend and that can be put to the experimental test. In the case of theology, it is the reality of God who transcends us and who can be met with only in awe and obedience. Once that distinction is understood, we can perceive the two disciplines to be intellectual cousins under the skin, despite the differences arising from their contrasting subject material.[6]

When theologians, then, cross the Jordan, they do so wearing the distinct camel's hair of their own field of study. To be sure, theologians can be careful, listening students of other disciplines, even though this does not call for them to abandon their own distinct way of working.

Another aspect of borderland theology is described by theologians as *liminality*. Coming into theology from the field of psychology, the word *liminal* expresses a notion or idea that is beginning to come into consciousness, as distinguished from something that is subliminal. Theologians have adopted this term when grappling with how human beings—especially those living between defined cultural realities—do the work of theology. A child born to Brazilian parents, for example, moves to France when she is a young child. Her parents speak Portuguese, and her friends speak French. Seeking to maintain their Brazilian identity, her family wants to celebrate Carnival in the early spring, though her French friends know nothing of this tradition, and the festival is limited to their own household, a vague shadow of what is happening in Rio de Janeiro. Living between these two cultural realities, we can say she is navigating a liminal space, a borderland between Brazilian and French culture.

---

[6]Polkinghorne, *Science and Theology*, 20.

Some theologians have suggested that liminality offers possibilities for creative theological work among the many challenges it presents. Offering a perspective from Asian American theology, Sang Hyun Lee vividly describes the experience of liminality as "dangling at the doorstep" of a new place. "Many Asian American individuals," he writes, "have important positions deep in the American structure, but only occupationally and not socio-politically. They, like other Asian Americans, are still in the wilderness of liminal in-betweenness, making regular visits to their workplaces, but without enjoying genuine human contact." Creatively, liminality "creates a framework within which participants can experiment with the familiar elements of normative social life, reconfiguring them in novel ways and discovering new arrangements and possibilities."[7] Unquestionably, that kind of work can be construed as disruptive and even chaotic because it does not fit neatly into any existing category and indeed presents a challenge.

The virtue exhibited in John the Baptist, taking up his ministry in the liminal borderland between wilderness and Jerusalem, reminds us that the announcement of the Lord's coming is going to be disruptive. At the same time, it also commends to us the liminal realities associated with the theological life. Theologians will often be called to do their work betwixt and between, to speak of God's redemption in ways that explode the boundaries of established categories.

Between promise and wilderness. Finally, the third aspect of John's theological geography is his situation between promise and wilderness. The work of theology is often edgy because it works at the leading edge of God's promise in the midst of wilderness. Wilderness, of course, was that untamed and menacing beyond, outside and past God's ordering goodness. It is striking, then, that John takes his ministry "beyond the Jordan." He is, of course, a precursor to Jesus, who is propelled by the Spirit into the wilderness just after John baptizes him (Mt 4:1; Lk 4:1). Similarly, Jesus crosses to the other side of the Sea of Galilee in Mark's graphic depiction we surveyed above.

---

[7]Sang Hyun Lee, *From a Liminal Space: An Asian American Theology* (Minneapolis: Fortress, 2010), 6-7-8.

In preparing the way of the Lord, then, John's theological virtue in the borderland is going to the wild and uncharted places. It is stepping to the edge of where God has established order and then stepping just beyond it, announcing the arrival of the one who will bring good order to all of creation. What does this mean for the work of theologians? It means we are those who are called, in the wilderness footsteps of John the Baptist, to courageously engage the places we might assume are devoid of God's presence. It is to engage the places that are in deep need of redemption.

This engagement, of course, calls us to remember how John did his work. Rather than announcing himself as savior, he continually pointed to the coming of another. Theologians of many stripes can be tempted to engage places as if our message were what will bring salvation. As John shows us, though, his proclamation is not what brings salvation. God's own presence is bringing peace, restoration, and salvation. In pointing toward the work of another, John exhibits a theological virtue of humility even as he engages the wilderness on the other side of the Jordan.

A bit of theology to round out these geographical reflections: Jesus' baptism is what propels him into the wilderness, "full of the Holy Spirit" (Lk 4:1). There, in the wilds beyond the Promised Land, he faces down the temptations that plagued his own people. Desire for security, desire for provision, desire for power—all of these are what Jesus confronts, straight out of his baptism. As a son of Israel and the Son of God, Jesus defeats all of these temptations. Filled by the Spirit out of our baptism, then, followers of Jesus can enter the wilderness under the promise that Jesus has overcome the very things that threatened to destroy God's people in the desert beyond the Jordan. In Jesus' baptismal action, the dynamics of the divine presence in the Promised Land spill over into the wilderness. When we step into the wilderness, then, we do so knowing that God is already present and working. We do not bring God's presence into the wilderness in our theological work; we announce what God is already doing and call others to join themselves to God's joyful, working presence.

The gift to us is that we follow not only John but also Jesus. Though we may, with John, be the voice of one crying out in the wilderness, that voice can now proclaim that the Son, in the power of the Spirit, has filled the wilderness with the redemptive presence of God. There is no wilderness space where God is not already present and active.

This reality expands with Jesus' entrance into the final wilderness of death. If wilderness is what threatens death, Jesus' entrance into death itself dispossesses wilderness of the last card it had to play. In his resurrection, Jesus does not escape death but goes *through* it to the other side. In his crucifixion and resurrection, he crosses the Jordan yet again, into the place of death, and comes through it, leaving it changed forever. Wherever we find the death-dealing dynamics of wilderness, then, the work of theology calls for us to join our voice to John's and cry out in the wilderness, proclaiming the goodness of God that is present, active, and full of life.

PRAYER

Gracious God who comes to save,
In your mercy, grant that I may be one to prepare the way for you.
Give me the wisdom, O God, to know how to make straight the paths
    for your presence
That every valley may be filled in and every mountain be made low
That every crooked road become straight
That every rough way would be made smooth
So that all people will see your salvation.
In your grace, strengthen me to stand at the edge.
Make me at home among those who are forgotten. May their testimony
    teach me of you.
Meet me in the wilderness, that I might be sustained by your holy
    presence, now and forever.
Amen.

QUESTIONS FOR DISCUSSION OR REFLECTION

1. How are you tempted to act as if the proclamation of theology were the offer of salvation itself? In what ways does John's humility challenge, convict, or encourage you?

2. Have you experienced a marginal position as a liability or an asset? How do you respond to the notion that theological virtue can be found outside the centers of cultural power? Does this comfort, challenge, or shift your work as a theologian?

3. Consider the three geographical elements of John's ministry: outside Jerusalem, in a border territory, between promise and wilderness. Can you locate your own experience in one or more of these realities? How does this shape an understanding of yourself as a theologian?

4. In what ways do you find theology to be edgy in your context? How is the proclamation of God disruptive, and how is it being received? What do you see as your role in that?

CHAPTER NINE

The Woman Who Anointed Jesus

ON LOVE

THE STORY OF THE WOMAN ANOINTING JESUS is one you can smell. The aroma of a woman's self-sacrifice is an olfactory testimony to the virtues of love and worship, a fragrant invitation to do theology as a breaking open of all we have to bring. Turning to a woman hunched at Jesus' feet breaches what we traditionally refer to as theology, because hers is a wordless act of offering. Still, in her story there is virtue to be found for doing the work of theology. A virtuous image of walking the theological life can be found in her, setting the work of theology in its proper place: a self-giving offering being poured out in love.

Examining this woman's sacrifice, however, will also invite us into an examination of the beautiful complexity of Christian Scripture. A version of this story appears in each of the four Gospels, one attributing the outpouring to Mary, the sister of Lazarus. Three times, the story is set in Bethany, while Luke tells a version that locates this event at a dinner Jesus is having at the house of a Pharisee. Rather than treat these as frustrating inconsistencies, we are going to use the opportunity to explore the ways theology works interactively from Scripture's often complex testimony. Our approach will be to tease out how different approaches to this story might shape our response to it and ask whether certain approaches to Scripture are more or less likely to help us to walk the theological life virtuously. Working theologically with Scripture, in other words, always calls for interpretative choices to be made, so we will welcome the complexity of this particular story as a means of developing an eye for biblical interpretation that is virtuously faithful for Christian life. First, though, we turn our attention to the astonishing theological work of a woman whose capacity to walk the theological life surprises especially those who could see in her nothing of virtue.

DO YOU SEE THIS WOMAN?

Calling the woman's anointing of Jesus theological work is delightfully disruptive. She offers no thoughtful treatise, nor a profound exposition on doctrine. She does, however, respond to the presence of Jesus with everything she has. Her response is an extravagant act of love for Jesus. "Do you see this woman?" Jesus asks his Pharisee host, a trained theologian. "I came into your house. You did not give me any water for my feet, but she wet my feet with her tears and wiped them with her hair. You did not give me a kiss, but this woman, from the time I entered, has not stopped kissing my feet" (Lk 7:44-45).

There is something in Jesus' response that goes beyond comparing Simon with this unnamed woman. Though it would be easy to read this account in tones of shame, Jesus' original question to his host moves us in a different direction. His question is especially poignant when addressed to trained theologians who are skilled in the art of knowing the things of God. Jesus does not tell Simon he has wasted his life on training himself to know God's law inside and out, of course, but he does reorient the room, bringing the woman's outpouring to the center of the conversation. "Do you see this woman?" Out of the many ways we could hear this question, it does not seem that Jesus asks it in shameful tones. There is, rather, something more genuine in what he asks, because Jesus truly wants Simon to see the woman who has entered his house and the virtues she now exhibits in her extravagant outpouring of love. "Therefore, I tell you, her many sins have been forgiven—as her great love has shown" (Lk 7:47).

Of course, judging by the way he has written this story, Luke probably would not mind if we did just a little comparison. He has, after all, set the story with these two distinctly different characters for us to see. With the woman on the one hand (or feet, as the case may be) and Simon on the other, we are pressed into asking where theological virtue is being exhibited. Is it in the actions of a man trained in all things theological and his capacity for upholding social norms? Or is it in the disruptive, extravagant act of love in a woman who cannot contain her gratitude? Simon's analytical skill is finely tuned; he can evaluate the woman's moral shortcomings and Jesus' prophetic qualifications in one eventful moment. Yet, the virtue of responding to Jesus lies elsewhere. Jesus lifts up the woman's virtue as she lets her tears fall down.

In essence, her orienting virtue is love, fueled by a desire for God. In her actions we see a burning passion that has driven her to the feet of Jesus, and she is holding nothing back. Her response to the presence of Jesus is to pour out everything she has. If only Simon could see—truly see!—this woman, as Jesus has requested. If he did, would he be able to see virtue? Could he look past her ethical questionability and see that she has exceeded his own virtue? If we target these questions to Simon alone, however, the power in this story may be lost on us. Do *we* see her? Do we have the theological vision to not only see the one who pours out herself in loving desire for Jesus but learn from and defer to her example? Could we really allow a woman with a morally dubious past who stands on the outskirts of society to reshape the way we do theology? Hear Jesus' question again: "Do you see this woman?"

Having the capacity to see those who lavish love on Jesus is vital to the work of theology. They are those to whom Jesus most likely needs to direct our attention. They are those who, in all likelihood, have not been invited to the dinner, those whose presence is surprising or shocking, those whose past of neglect, abandonment, addiction, trauma, racism, or abuse has exacted an unwarranted toll from their very flesh, but they have come to lavish love on Jesus. *See* them. Look for them, for where you find them, there you will find Jesus in their midst.

These sons and daughters are not a theological means to an end, however. We do not look *at* them as if we were methodological voyeurs, gazing at them for our own benefit, but *to* them as respected teachers, vital to the life of the church. In the community of Jesus, those who lavish love on our Lord amend our impulses and call for faithfulness by their witness. Theological method is to be measured according to faithfulness to Christ, and he is calling us to see them, holding them up as exemplars of virtue. See how they love Jesus, and then see whether the way you approach the work of theology remains unaffected. If you do theology while ignoring those who have been pressed out in shame, do not be surprised when Jesus readjusts everything by directing your attention to them and calling for your method to adjust to account for their faithfulness. "Do you see this woman?"

It is not only what Jesus says, however, that calls our attention to theological virtue. The woman's witness—her outpouring of love—is also a virtue that Jesus does not want the rest of their companions to miss. Hers is the virtue of love. It is the virtue of centering desire on its proper theological object and allowing the rest of life to flow by that arrangement. It is the virtue of a heart locked on its true center.

PASSION, LOVE, AND THEOLOGY

Though love and desire tend to be treated as passing emotional states, only secondarily related to serious theological work, theologians have long found them to be essential to our particular kind of work. "Without love," Karl Barth instructs those beginning their theological studies, "theological work would be a miserable polemics and a waste of words."[1] What else could rescue us more effectively from the misery

---

[1] Karl Barth, *Evangelical Theology: An Introduction* (Grand Rapids, MI: Eerdmans, 1963), 197.

of loveless polemics but a woman pouring out her tears on Jesus' feet? The all-encompassing love expressed in this woman's action is the life-blood of theology.

Her example, then, is invigorating to theological work, especially when the earthy and earnest passions that are stirred in the life of faith are treated with suspicion. Even Barth, who championed love as essential to the work of theology, seems to be uncomfortable with the amount of passion we find in a story like this. "Love, as Eros," he writes, "is, in general terms, the primordially powerful desire, urge, impulse, and endeavor by which a created being seeks his own self-assertion, satisfaction, realization, and fulfillment in his relation to something else." The pulsing power in Barth's description is unmistakable for anyone who has longed for something or someone. This impulse, though, can also relate to knowledge, according to Barth, in what he refers to as scientific *eros*. "It is the soaring movement by which human knowledge lets itself be borne toward its objects and hurries toward them in order to unite them with itself and itself with them, to bring them into its possession and power, and to enjoy them in this way."[2] In light of Barth's description and the misshapen desire that lurks around the edges of theology to lust after knowledge rather than longing for the God who knows, Jesus' question redirects our attention to one whose love is aimed well: "Do you see this woman?"

As if instructed by Jesus' question, Barth goes on to caution that scientific *eros* can be directed either toward God or toward humanity. If directed toward God, theology becomes the fuel burning hot for the beauty of holiness; if directed toward humanity, theology can become the vain and empty pursuit of one's own glory. Eventually, Barth names the reality that *eros* is not a native term to the New Testament. Indeed, the love Jesus affirms in the woman is communicated by Luke as *agapē*, the term Barth turns to examine. Even while acknowledging that *eros* and *agapē* share the notion of "the total seeking of another," Barth makes

---

[2]Barth, *Evangelical Theology*, 197-98.

the unfortunate claim that *agapē* "signifies a movement which runs almost exactly in the opposite direction from that of Eros."[3]

Setting up *agapē* and *eros* as opposites is not unfortunate in philosophical or categorical terms, necessarily. The distinction Barth is seeking to make reflects his characteristic method of *dialectical theology*, in which human life is understood as existence within the tension between two opposing realities, especially the Word of God and the fallen creation. The woman at Jesus' feet, though, seems to know little of this tension. For her, *eros* and *agapē* find unity in Jesus. Her love is pure, and it is passionate. These do not rage against one another inside her; the virtue we find in her life is that erotic (*eros*) and self-giving (*agapē*) love are filled out by each other as she lavishes total love on Jesus.[4] She longs to be near him, precisely because her central motivation is to give to Jesus in an act of self-sacrifice. *Agapē*, Mildred Bangs Wynkoop reminds us, "is a quality of person rather than a different kind of love. It is a principle by which one orders life—or by which love is ordered." Wynkoop goes on to instruct, "Agape cannot be defined, but it can be demonstrated."[5] The woman at Jesus' feet is an exemplar in her demonstration.

Deferring to this woman's testimony helps us beyond setting *eros* and *agapē* as opposites, a move that would make it difficult for us to see her as a teacher of theological virtue. Setting *eros* against *agapē* codifies in our imaginations that there is little room for passionate love in the theological life. Responding to Jesus' request to see the woman, however, reminds us that passionate love finds a true home when it is directed toward Christ. Instructed by her virtuous love, we see that theology calls for us to love passionately and to love sacrificially, *eros* filled out by *agapē*.

Theologian Sarah Coakley's work offers a still fuller account of the relationship between these two. She is critical of approaches to love that

---

[3]Barth, *Evangelical Theology*, 200.
[4]Note that erotic and sexual can be distinguished. Erotic love primarily deals with passionate, even fleshly desire. While sexual desire can certainly fit that description, erotic desire can move beyond sexual desire.
[5]Mildred Bangs Wynkoop, *A Theology of Love: The Dynamic of Wesleyanism* (Kansas City, MO: Beacon Hill, 2015), 37, 40.

cast *agapē* and *eros* as dichotomously opposed realities wherein "Christian *agape* draws one upwards, and the selfish Greek *eros* downwards." Coakley convincingly argues that Christianity as early as the second and third centuries reverberated with Greek notions of desire so that, "although it could find little or nothing in Jesus's teachings about *eros* as such, it did not read his views on love (*agape*) as in any way disjunctive from the Platonic tradition of *eros*."[6] Or, as Philip Crill and James McCullough write, "*Eros* is often imagined to be the opposite of *agape* (often misunderstood rather blandly as 'disinterested love'), but in Christ the concept of *eros* itself is redeemed."[7]

Coakley's reminder that Christian theology has long held together passionate desire with love shines a virtuous light on the woman at Jesus' feet. She is no shame-bound outcast; indeed, her passionate love for Jesus is *agapē* and *eros* united in its true center. Though Simon is quick to identify her as one whose sins have caused her to miss the mark, "her many sins have been forgiven—as her great love has shown" precisely because her love is fulfilled by its Christocentric direction.

Her actions, then, teach us deeply about theological virtue. Before her mouth speaks in doctrinal oration or sermonic performance, it kisses Jesus' feet. Her hands do not busy themselves writing essays or treatises because they are blotting her tear-drenched hair to his toes. Quite simply, she will not stop lavishing fulfilled love on Jesus. Jesus' question, then, confronts those of us who are seeking to posture ourselves for virtuous theological work: "Do you see this woman?"

SHE HAS DONE A BEAUTIFUL THING

This passionate, even erotic account signals a virtue of the theological life. The theological life can be a passionate affair. The love the woman lavishes on Jesus is a beautiful thing, he says, anointing him for his

---

[6]Sarah Coakley, *God, Sexuality, and the Self: An Essay "On the Trinity"* (Cambridge: Cambridge University Press, 2013), 30, 8.

[7]Philip Krill and James McCullough, *Life in the Trinity: The Mystery of God and Human Deification* (Eugene, OR: Wipf & Stock, 2022), 96.

death or, as we sometimes refer to it, his passion. Yet, theology sometimes carries a connotation that it should not be done passionately.
Often we have made it out to be a decidedly dispassionate enterprise, an
exercise in severing the head from the heart. It is a rational kind of work,
we are told.

I am not challenging the notion that theology is supposed to be rational; what I am challenging is rationality's disconnection from passion.
I am doing this not because it is simply a more enjoyable way to approach
theology but specifically because the very life of God is love and passion.
What if theology operated in full account of this passionate, loving God?
What if it were done in full acknowledgment and submission to communion with a passionate God? Put another way, what if the theological
life were nothing short of being taken up into the dynamic, passionate
life of love that is God's Trinity?

Admittedly, this is where the line between doctrine itself and method
gets a little fuzzy. A lot of insightful theology has been produced on the
nature of God's trinitarian life of love, and I hope you will find your way
to those beautiful contributions. My point here is that theology is at full
stretch when it responds to God in the way that God has chosen to address us. If God addresses us by opening the life of love and inviting us
to join, what might that do to the shape of our theological response? The
Father, who eternally loves the Son in the Spirit, and the Son, who eternally returns love to the Father in the Spirit, constitute the life of God,
which is nothing other than love itself. When that life graciously opens
to us, when it offers us an invitation to enter in and be caught up, what
else could our response be but passionate? "We are not commanded or
forced by Christ to enter into the Trinitarian embrace," Krill and Mc-
Cullough remind us, "we are invited. Christ desires followers who experience the same longing, yearning, and desire for him that characterize
his own burning love for the Father." The woman whose witness guides
us in this chapter was neither commanded nor forced to do what she did,
but in the lavishness of her response, we find a passionate, beautiful response. "Jesus wants disciples who love him affectionately, aspiringly

indeed, *erotically*," Krill and McCullough continue. "He praised the sinful woman who washes his feet with her tears."[8]

If theology is a response to God's activity, and I agree that it is, the virtue this woman commends to us is to let it be a full, passionate response of love. We need not check our passion at the door to respond to the invitation to theology. While there will always be a call to clarity and logical relationships in theology, all of that can live quite nicely alongside a longing desire to pour our best on the feet of the one who evokes such a powerful description.

THE USE OF SCRIPTURE "IN MEMORY OF HER"

We turn now to a somewhat different set of questions that show up around this woman and her story, namely, the challenges that arise from four different tellings, with all their differences. Jesus remarks that wherever the gospel is proclaimed, the woman's sacrificial outpouring will be told, "in memory of her" (Mt 26:13; Mk 14:9). Luke and John do not include this but emphasize other kinds of themes around the event. The diversity in their witness gives us an opportunity to reflect not only on how theology deals with these kinds of differences but on how theology arises from Scripture in virtuous ways. Many introductory books on theological method include some instruction on the use of Scripture, and we will do some of that now. Turning to this particular story, though, allows us to do that with an eye to a particular theological virtue, which is the love of Jesus centralizing the story. In other words, we will consider some methodological implications for using Scripture in theology in memory of this woman and the beauty of what she did.

Let us begin, then, with an overview of the way the Gospel writers each treat this story. Table 9.1 below highlights some of each passage's unique characteristics regarding a woman anointing Jesus while also demonstrating how differences emerge from book to book.

---

[8]Krill and McCullough, *Life in the Trinity*, 96, 99.

Table 9.1. Variance in the Story of the Woman Who Anointed Jesus

Matthew 26:6-13	Mark 14:3-9	Luke 7:36-50	John 12:1-8
Perfume is poured out on Jesus' head	Perfume is poured out on Jesus' head	Perfume is poured out on Jesus' feet	Perfume is poured out on Jesus' feet
Location is identified as Bethany, at the home of Simon the leper	Location is identified as Bethany, at the home of Simon the leper	Location is identified as the home of a Pharisee, whom Jesus calls Simon; no city is identified	Location is identified as Bethany; Martha serves, but the exact house is not identified; no one named Simon or any Pharisees are identified
The woman is unnamed; no moral status is given	The woman is unnamed; no moral status is given	The woman is unnamed; we learn she "lived a sinful life," though the nature of the sin is not named	The woman is identified as Mary, the sister of Lazarus; no moral status is given

As is often the case, Matthew agrees with Mark not only on the substance but also on many of the details. In this case, both concur that the woman's anointing was connected to Jesus' impending death and burial. Her story flows quickly toward Jesus' arrest, trial, and crucifixion. Jesus' response, too, highlights her work as preparation for his death.

Traditionally understood to be written after Mark and Matthew, Luke expands on the first two Gospels with his own distinctive themes of Gentile inclusion while also locating the story far earlier in his account of Jesus' ministry. For Luke, two-thirds of his Gospel unfolds after the woman anoints Jesus. John, the account most scholars agree was written last, sets the aromatic account alongside the raising of Lazarus from the dead, a story he alone offers.

What are we to make of these differences? Is this the same story with differences emerging across time, or are we dealing with accounts of multiple women who anoint Jesus? Do these variances expose a fault line so deep that it shakes the confidence of theologians in using Scripture in their work? Further still, are these differences, as some critics of the Bible charge, yet another example of how its ancient mystique simply cannot be trusted in a modern world?

As we move toward a brief but important survey of methodologies concerning Scripture, I am going to call your attention to an image that

I hope will be a guide of sorts. Consider the image of the woman crumpled at the feet of Jesus. In Luke's account, particularly, there seems to be a lot going on around her, but Jesus remains central to her focus and activity.

With that image in mind, let us begin to ask about the approaches to and uses of Scripture that allow Jesus to remain central. There is, of course, a kind of theological virtue in what I am proposing: an approach to Scripture that primarily seeks to know the God to whom these sets of texts are bearing witness. This image can guide us not only in how we deal with Scripture itself but also in the ways we make use of Scripture in the work of theology. Holding that image in mind, then, let us begin with how Scripture can be used in theology.

SCRIPTURE AND THE SOURCES OF THEOLOGY

Typically, theologians have identified several sources of theological knowledge. Scripture tends to rank first among them, followed by tradition, reason, and experience. Some theologians will treat these as relative equals (often giving Scripture the leading edge), using a method in which we come to knowledge through one source that needs to be verified by the others. We may have an experience, for example, that seems persuasive but needs to be verified according to Scripture, reason, and tradition. In a network of verification, they tend to work together to offer us deeper theological knowledge.

A variation on this is the notion that Scripture is the primary source among these four and that the remaining three are helpful tools, allowing us to insightfully interpret and unpack Scripture. Acknowledging that every encounter with Scripture is being interpreted in one way or another, we consciously use these tools to provide a more vivid understanding. When we come to a passage of the Bible, then, we can ask of tradition, "What have other Christians said about this across the years? How can their insights help me?" Of reason, we can ask, "What interpretative tools can I use here to expand or correct my knowledge?" As for experience, we might find a kind of check to verify what we might have found through the application of reason or an appeal to tradition.

To be sure, these approaches offer a lot of merit and are in wide use in contemporary theology. I do want to point out, however, how these kinds of approaches may tend toward theological knowledge as a data set. That is, these methods can be helpful at delivering to us knowledge in the form of information. We might determine something to be true if we can verify it as a matter of fact through applying the method I have just outlined. It is at this point that the image of the woman at Jesus' feet calls us to consider these methods in memory of her. There was no bit of information on which she would have poured out expensive perfume. Only Jesus—the living God in the flesh—was worthy of her sacrifice. This is not to say that the methods I have outlined above cannot produce a relational, dynamic knowledge of a living God, but it is to hold up in our memory this woman and the virtue of seeking after the living God. When we go to Scripture, are we after information about God, or are we seeking intimate knowledge of the living God to whom these texts testify?

When I was making my way through the turbulent years of high school, I remember a friend expressing a crush on a new student who had transferred to our school. A mutual friend of ours went to work, collecting as much information about the recent arrival as she could. Her week-long fact-finding mission culminated in a three-by-five notecard, filled with facts about the new student, from her favorite color to her shoe size. I can still recall the look of satisfaction on our friend's face when she presented it to our twitterpated companion. Bewildered, he held the card, looked at it, and said, "What am I supposed to do with this?" It was clear that receiving information *about* his crush was not going to be the same as getting to know *her*.

Sometimes our tendency in theology is to go to Scripture as if it were a bank of facts about the one who has drawn our attention. Theology can sometimes become a bit like collecting as many facts as we can about the living God and then presenting them to those whose hearts yearn to know God in a deeply relational way. The virtuous act of the woman at Jesus' feet is an enduring reminder that information *about* this living God will not be a substitute for love that unites us with a living reality. She would not have been satisfied with learning about Jesus. Her impulse was to make her way into his very presence, knowing him through the logic of love. Gladly, Scripture functions according to similar logic. It welcomes theologians who will not be satisfied with knowing *about* God because they see something broader is opening to them. Through the enlivening of God's own presence, Scripture invites us to know the God who is speaking. This is a reality we refer to as *inspiration*, and the image of the woman at Jesus' feet will help us explore this as well.

GOD'S BREATHING

The notion of inspiration (literally, *in-spirit-ation*) offers a thrilling array of theological possibility, precisely because from top to bottom it is a testimony to what God does to bring Scripture to life and bring us to life through the reading of Scripture. After all, bringing things to life is what God's Spirit tends to do, so if we turn to these ancient texts expecting them to be dusty, we should not be surprised when the Spirit of God brings that dust to life. Because of God's presence, we read these texts in the company of those first humans, who are nothing other than God-breathed dust. We read Scripture listening for the rattling of dry bones, because God's question to Ezekiel is issued through the same Spirit who enlivens us: "Can these bones live?" (Ezek 37:3). The new thing that began at the Spirit's movement at Pentecost continues right through the reading today, not because these are magical words but because the life-giving God is dynamically present, meeting us in the reading of these God-breathed words. This means, then, that the same Spirit who inspired the biblical writers continues to illuminate their words as we read them now. God not only enlivened Scripture's writing long ago but continues to bring life to its reading today. In the end, then, we can see that Scripture is not really about Scripture at all; it is about the God who is still speaking, calling, summoning to a dynamic and intimate knowledge of the holy.

What does this mean, then, for all those differences we found in the story of the woman anointing Jesus? Are the critics who say the Bible is full of contradictions correct? Are these differences a fracture to the credibility of the Bible's use in theology?

A couple of general approaches emerge when we look at the way different Christian theological traditions have discussed inspiration. While many traditions affirm the *plenary inspiration* of Scripture, meaning that all of the texts selected for canonization in the Bible are inspired by God, there is some difference among theological traditions on *how* all of Scripture is inspired.

Some traditions take a *verbal inspiration* approach, which affirms that the Holy Spirit worked in a close relational sense with the biblical writers, so that when the writers took pen in hand, their close relationship with the Spirit guided the writing in its content. We might think of the way couples who have been married for decades tell stories, especially when they are both in the room at the time. If you listen carefully, you can detect that the way each thinks about the story and recalls it has been deeply influenced by the other. In the case of verbal inspiration, the biblical writers are thought to have maintained such a close relationship with the Holy Spirit that the relationship influenced but did not dictate every word they wrote.

Dictation theory, on the other hand, maintains that the Holy Spirit told the biblical writers what to write, word for word. Some theological methods that place strong emphasis on *theological epistemology*, the study of how we come to know theological realities, will often gravitate toward dictation theory, largely because it strongly affirms that every word in the Bible was dictated by God directly. Churches that begin their official statement of belief with Scripture are usually trying to communicate something about the epistemological viability of the Bible. Their methodological reasoning often falls along the lines of establishing trust in Scripture's viability and trustworthiness first, so that the content contained therein can serve as the foundation of theological reasoning. Our ability to affirm belief in God, then, largely rests on being able to trust the vehicle through which this knowledge is communicated. Often, this means affirming that not only is Scripture entirely inspired but that the biblical writers were inspired in such a way that every word they wrote was dictated to them by God.

This brief account, of course, cannot account for all the nuance and diversity of the ways various traditions work with Scripture, but it gives us a glimpse behind the methodological curtain to see the way we might approach Scripture, especially considering the differences in the stories of the woman who anointed Jesus.

The differences in the stories about the woman at Jesus' feet may present challenges to those who approach Scripture as if it were attempting to provide a detailed account of Jesus' life and ministry. If the details are off, this challenge goes, we should not trust the source because it is not "true." Generally, this kind of account is smuggling in a presupposition about truth, namely that truth is found in the verifiability of certain facts—the data sets we discussed earlier. Modern disciplines such as journalism and science function this way, for good reason. Ancient thinkers, however, did not always live with these commitments. While they undoubtedly wanted to communicate the truth, they did not find the truth to be locked into the details of *exactly* the way something happened. John's Gospel, for example, locates the story of Jesus expelling moneychangers from the temple in the second chapter of his account, while the Synoptic writers present this event toward the end of the story, as one of the catalysts leading directly to Jesus' arrest, trial, and crucifixion. Does this mean that John's account is not true? Taking his way of truth telling into account will help us, because from the opening words of his Gospel, John is signaling that he is telling the story of Jesus in light of (new) creation. Rather than presenting the stories in direct chronological order, John wants us to see how Jesus' actions reveal the way God is re-creating, setting right what has gone wrong in a fallen creation. John is telling us the truth that Jesus is making all things new, and he has rearranged some of the chronological details to be able to tell us that truth. When we impose modern epistemologies on ancient texts—when we try to make the Bible tell us the truth exclusively as a modern journalist would, for example—we bump into several challenges around passages such as Jesus cleansing the temple or the woman at Jesus' feet.

This is precisely where the woman at Jesus' feet may offer us a virtuous move that results in a methodological gift. She is one who came seeking *Jesus*. Rather than information about him, she came driven by a passionate desire to know him. If we join her in her approach, perhaps these differences do not present a challenge to Scripture's viability at all. Perhaps all of these accounts are helping us to know Jesus in a richer, more nuanced way. Luke's account, for example, is telling us the truth about *Jesus*, especially regarding Jesus' proclivity to welcome outsiders, such as Gentiles. His emphasis on the woman's "sinful life," a detail not included in any of the other Gospel accounts, reminds us of the truth about Jesus' hospitality to those who have lived sin-filled lives. His forgiveness of the woman's sins at the end of the passage, verbal-theory advocates would affirm, tells us the truth about Jesus' nature and how he offers welcome to outsiders. At the same time, a verbal-theory approach would account for John's vastly different account of this encounter by recognizing John's placement of this story directly before Jesus enters Jerusalem to shouts of "Hosanna!" Mary's anointing of Jesus with perfume is at the same time a preparation for his burial and his coronation as king. John, too, though telling it differently, is telling the truth about Jesus' kingship: it will come through his death.

By placing Jesus at the center of her love, the woman at his feet offers us a kind of virtue that allows us to joyfully work with Scripture as the inspired Word of God that invites us to know the one who said of himself that he is "the way and the truth and the life" (Jn 14:6). Her example allows us to not only read Scripture with a passion for God but to also to proclaim with Paul, "I want to know Christ," not only *about* Christ (Phil 3:10). Her example rescues theology from presenting facts about a distant reality and instead offers a method by which our intimate acquaintance with the holy God who became flesh makes sense of our passionate love.

The overarching point is that a theology of inspiration reminds us that when we read the Bible, we are encountering not only words on a page but the living God who is made manifest by the third person of the Trinity. In other words, we do not only read the Bible for its own sake but for the sake of encountering the God to whom the Bible points and testifies. "One of the main tasks of theology," John Webster writes, "is to exemplify and promote close and delighted reading of Holy Scripture as the *viva vox Dei*, the voice of the risen Jesus to his community."[9] If, in our work as theologians, we forget that Scripture is the enlivened and enlivening means by which the gospel is known, we risk not seeing this woman, who reminds us that seeking *Jesus* passionately is a theological virtue that can gladly illuminate our reading of Scripture.

To be clear, Scripture is not an object of worship, for God alone is worthy of worship. Scripture, though, is the God-breathed gift given to the church that we might be caught up in its story and find ourselves in its pages. Theology, then, is not simply distilling doctrinal data from ancient texts but an exhilarating work of cracking alabaster jars open against the holiness of the living God.

JARS POURED OUT

When Jesus said that we would remember this woman wherever the gospel was proclaimed, I imagine that he saw something in her virtuous action that allowed the gospel to be proclaimed faithfully. Her method of emptying her jar may be a vehicle through which good news moves. This kind of outpouring, destabilizing, loving work, of course, is nothing short of living the gospel, because the gospel is the news of God's redemptively disruptive entrance into the world, an announcement that leaves no aspect of human life undisturbed. Among the many things we may want to hold tightly, be they ideas of God, ideas of the church, the latest trend in ministry, political commitments, or social positions, theology's work includes the call to continually dispossess whatever

---

[9]John Webster, *The Culture of Theology*, ed. Ivor J. Davidson and Alden C. McCray (Grand Rapids, MI: Baker Academic, 2019), 64.

we hold precisely because there is nothing we love more than God in Jesus Christ.

One of the most common forms of this is when someone makes a theological statement that begins with something like, "Because God is like this, then God *must* do that." Oftentimes phrases like this reveal some kind of theological commitment we have brought to an encounter with Jesus. Throughout my years of teaching theology, I have watched students struggle to reconcile Jesus' actions and teachings with the concepts of God they have brought to the task of theology. Sometimes they will go to extreme lengths to make sure that Jesus' actions—such as being subject to crucifixion, for example—fit into whatever theological concepts they have started with.

Some of Christianity's earliest theological confessions are the result of confronting these kinds of methods. The Apostles' Creed, for example, perhaps the earliest confession of the Christian faith we have, points out that Jesus was born of the Virgin Mary and suffered under Pontius Pilate. It seems odd that the only other humans mentioned in the creed beyond Jesus are Mary and Pilate. Mary plays a large part in the story, while Pilate seems to play a much smaller role. Their inclusion in the creed, though, was to affirm that Jesus really was born (represented by Mary) and that he really did suffer and die (represented by Pilate). These affirmations are nothing short of the early church's critique of Gnosticism, a blend of Platonism and early Christianity, which could not conceive of a God who was born or suffered. The nature of divinity, Gnostics contended, was that it was above or beyond bodily things such as suffering and dying. Gnostic thought went to lengths to explain how Jesus was divine but did not actually suffer and was not actually involved in something as bodily as childbirth. The early church's response: "You're holding too tightly to notions of divinity that you've brought to the conversation. Break them open on this encounter we've had with Jesus and see what kind of notions of divinity come out on the other side. Hold nothing back."

It is a common struggle to take some of our most closely held beliefs and pour them out on an encounter with Jesus, and yet this is a virtue of the theological life. For Christian theologians, even our concepts of God must be poured out in relationship to Jesus, for Jesus reveals to us the very nature of God. If we must do intellectual backflips to make our notions of God fit what we see in Jesus, we probably have a methodological problem on our hands. If we are committed to ideas that make Jesus seem inconsistent with divinity, the chances are high that we are holding on to something we love more than Jesus, and we would do well to pour it out in an act of love.

This is precisely how the virtue of pouring out everything on Jesus can be helpful to our method. Without adopting this woman's virtue, a theologian's capacity to speak the gospel will be muted because our lips will be kissing something other than Jesus. Holding on to these treasured things can be a way to retain the stability we often crave, the things that set our world in order. But that kind of stability is not a virtue of the theological life, precisely because the gospel is the announcement of a new creation in Jesus Christ.

This woman's example goes a long way in shaking us loose from the temptation in theology, whether pastoral, academic, or otherwise, to do our work by holding on to precious things. Her witness asks us to contemplate whether there is anything we are holding that we refuse to pour out on Jesus. If there is, we can be assured we love it more than Jesus, and it will undoubtedly shape our theology as it becomes a false object of worship. But here, crumpled at the feet of Jesus, is a masterful teacher, because there is nothing this woman loves more than the one who is making the world new. Guided by her longing for Jesus, the contents of her jar are set in their proper place. Like Paul, whose passionate longing to know Christ made his theological commitments and pedigree rubbish by comparison, her example exposes any impulse to withhold even those things we value most from being poured out on Jesus in an act of utter devotion, thanksgiving, and trust. Her love for Jesus is a living critique of methods that carry around our commitments, positions, and worldviews to Jesus but fail to pour them out. Jesus hoped Simon would see it if he would see the woman: the theological virtue of pouring out every commitment on Jesus.

We can, of course, resist her disruptive act. We can, with Simon, dismiss her in favor of the stable social system we know, the same system that made her an intruder rather than a guest. But the undeniable radicality of Jesus' ministry will open another way forward. His way unites her action with the proclamation of the gospel, precisely because this news will appear good only for those who empty their jars.

There, then, is the alternative possibility that stands open to us. We can, with this woman, set our love on its true center and shatter our jars of alabaster on the gospel. This woman's destabilizing, even intrusive presence summons theologians to do the jar-breaking, destabilizing work of gospel proclamation. That will mean, of course, that a virtue of the theological life is to continually break open whatever we might possess in an act of love on Jesus, so that the fragrance of the gospel might fill the room. It is, with this woman, to recognize God's entrance into the world through Jesus and reorient everything around this astoundingly good news. In her memory and according to her virtue, we learn to do the work of theology. For her, no jar will remain unbroken.

PRAYER

Gracious and loving God,

We confess that we have come to you holding tightly to that which is
    not you.

By your mercy, forgive us and renew us, drawing us close to your
    presence through your Son, Jesus Christ.

Remind us in your gentle way that you are pleased with those who
    worship at your feet.

Make us, though your Holy Spirit, to be delighted there.

Stir in us a love for you that defines who we are, that we may love you
    with a holy love

And that we may love our neighbors as ourselves,

To your glory forever and ever.

Amen.

QUESTIONS FOR DISCUSSION OR REFLECTION

1. Which would best characterize your theological journey: seeking information about Jesus or a passionate pursuit to know Jesus? What would it look like to defer to the woman's example of passionate love, and how might that shape the kind of theological work you are doing?

2. Have you encountered the tendency to divide *eros* and *agapē*, or passion and rationality? What would it look like to unite the two within your own life and theological work?

3. How do you respond to the idea that theological work is a continual call to dispossess whatever we hold? Can you identify anything you're holding onto that you may need to pour out? (Discerning what and how we let these things go often requires dialogue with a trusted friend, mentor, or spiritual director.)

CHAPTER TEN

Thomas

ON DOUBTING

IN ONE OF THE LESS FORTUNATE TURNS of Christian history, Thomas "is the disciple who has been known these last millennia only by his doubting."[1] It is not that doubt itself is unfortunate, as we will explore shortly. Rather, making Thomas into "Doubting Thomas" tends to collapse his theological journey to a single point along the line of his development. His journey is far more complex and instructive than we see when we reduce him to Doubting Thomas. We turn to Thomas, then, not only to teach us about the role of doubt in the work of theology but also to learn about doubt along the theological journey. Thomas is a man who calls us to reexamine our impulse to name certainty a virtue and doubt its corresponding vice. Doubt, he shows us, can be a virtue in the work of theology if we learn from him how to employ it well.

When we meet Thomas, he is anything but a doubter. John's Gospel gives us this first glimpse of Thomas as the Twelve are fervently debating the wisdom of what Jesus has just proposed they do (Jn 11:1-16). Lazarus, the friend of Jesus, has taken ill in Bethany, and it is not looking good for multiple reasons. First, Lazarus's illness seems to be serious enough that his sister would send word to Jesus to come quickly. Those are never the messages you want to receive. Making

---

[1]Jennifer Michael Hecht, *Doubt: A History* (San Francisco: HarperOne, 2003), 180.

matters more complicated, though, is that Bethany is in a place filled with people who are intent on killing Jesus. Going to Lazarus is a suicide mission, and Jesus' friends are quick to remind him of that. Except Thomas.

EARNEST ZEAL AND HONEST QUESTIONS

The way John tells it, Thomas does not speak until he is ready to go to Bethany and die. "Let us also go, that we may die with him," Thomas says (Jn 11:16). It has never been entirely clear to me whether Thomas is talking about Jesus or Lazarus. Does he want to die alongside Jesus if the blood-thirsty Judeans get their way and stone Jesus to death? Or is this something that lives more in the flow of John's theological message, such that Thomas wants to die with Lazarus so that he can also be awakened to a new kind of belief, a foreshadowing of what will take place when Thomas ultimately comes to a new depth of belief?[2] Maybe the truth in this encounter is big enough to hold both possibilities. Maybe John is intentionally vague to be able to make space for both.

What is not vague is John's presentation of Thomas as zealous. While each of the other Gospel writers give Thomas only the mention of his name in the list of the Twelve, John introduces him in a flash of ardent certainty. It may be that he was ready to be stoned to death alongside Jesus, and it may be that he was willing to die to be brought to new belief. Either way, this was a young man who was willing to die and was encouraging those around him to do the same. That does not strike me as someone who dabbled in doubt.

It does strike me, however, as being a lot like many of the people who are originally attracted to theological study. Full of zeal and willing to die if necessary, they are prepared to follow Jesus into tough situations and are not too keen on those who hesitate to do the same. It could be

---

[2]John's use of the same Greek root (*pistis*) in both Jn 11:15 and Jn 20:27 makes this a credible possibility. Jesus' invitation to Thomas to believe in Jn 20:27 is possibly the fulfillment of his hopes for the disciples in awakening Lazarus. In fact, the disciples are awakened to belief in seeing Jesus raise Lazarus from the dead, just as Thomas will ultimately be awakened to belief by seeing Jesus raised from the dead.

that I am overstating the case a bit. Maybe these are the folks who are attracted to theological exploration because they desire new discovery and are passionately in love with Jesus. They may not have a completely clear picture of what theology is, but if it is a way to know Jesus better, they are in for it. A potent mixture of certainty, zeal, and an intense desire to follow Jesus can drive us to theology, even before we know what theology is.

Perhaps that is why it can be so disorienting when the questions come. Some of the most zealous people I know approach theology with skepticism, because theology is so often associated with questions, and questions can be cast as the enemy of certainty.

On this, though, Thomas has something to teach us about the work of theology. When we next encounter him, he is full of questions, and he is not shy about asking them. The setting for this questioning confrontation is Jesus beginning to discuss his departure with the disciples. Of course, this is John's account, so the language is dripping with theological significance. The scene opens with Jesus using that same word for belief that hovers around every one of Thomas's appearances in the Gospel. "You believe in God," Jesus tells them. "Believe also in me" (Jn 14:1). Maybe it was being told to believe that set Thomas off. Maybe it simply got him thinking or even frustrated. Jesus, I am sure, had conversations with his disciples that were gentle in demeanor and placid in tone, but I am not nearly as sure this was one of them. When Jesus finally tells his disciples, "You know the way to the place I am going," Thomas cannot hold his tongue any longer (Jn 14:4).

"Lord, we don't know where you are going, so how can we know the way?" (Jn 14:5). It may not be how he said it, but I hear Thomas's question in the tone of a frustrated and disoriented theology student whose certainty is beginning to be penetrated by questions. It is not that Thomas is rejecting what Jesus has to say, but gone are the days of him jumping at the chance to die without asking a single question. My paraphrase of Thomas goes like this: "That doesn't make sense! You haven't even told us where you're going, so how on earth can you expect us to know how to get there?" People called Jesus "Good Teacher," but you can get frustrated even with someone who is good at teaching.

I have an affinity for Thomas's question because it resembles someone who has been at the work of theology long enough to start asking honest questions. It is not that the unquestioning zeal of the beginning stages is bad, but Thomas is beginning to demonstrate that taking questions directly to Jesus is just as much a part of the theological journey as is zealous obedience.

ASKING HONEST QUESTIONS

Thomas reminds us that asking honest questions—even those asked in a bit of frustration—is a vital and legitimate part of walking the theological life. The trouble is that in a culture that prizes certainty, questions can often come off like a rejection of the faith altogether. Notice Thomas here. He has serious questions about what Jesus said, but he is not necessarily giving up on following Jesus. In fact, Thomas's question sets Jesus up to make one of the most profound statements in any of the Gospels: "I am the way and the truth and the life" (Jn 14:6). Thomas's honest question provokes a revelation of truth about Jesus that speaks to the most significant questions of human life. Here, in this turning point, questions of truth pivot from being informational and cognitive to personal. As it turns out, truth never consisted of bits of information but the person of Jesus himself. As it turns out, truth itself did not mind being questioned because when truth is probed, it gives you more of itself. Thomas's honest questions only lead to a deeper knowledge of truth.

Questions have the possibility to lead us toward the goodness of truth in the person of Jesus, and Thomas teaches us that moving from zealous certainty toward questions is a virtue of the theological life. If this is a difficult lesson for us to learn from Thomas, it is probably because we rarely associate questions or doubt with theological virtue, at least when we are starting out. In short, we have come to associate questions with the one thing Jesus seems to want his disciples to get past: unbelief. It is a hang-up that Thomas does not have, though, and his

approach helps us to question an immediate connection between unbelief and doubt. Doubt, as Casey Tygrett puts it, is sometimes "curiosity cast as a villain."[3]

In his questioning, Thomas de-vilifies doubt because he shows us that
his questions produce new depths of understanding. In his thoughtful
instructions to seminary students beginning their theological studies,
renowned theologian Karl Barth says, "Doubt springs from the theological necessity of treating the quest for truth as a task that is never
completed."[4] Indeed, as we seek to know God, we are seeking to know
an inexhaustible source of goodness. In theology, there will always be
more to learn. Honest questions can help us in that learning. Any danger
associated with doubt is not in the asking of questions but in giving up
the quest.

A third and final appearance in John's Gospel rounds out our journey
with Thomas (Jn 20:24-28). It is the last substantial interaction we have
with him, and it is the interaction that has associated him with doubt for
generations. The scene unfolds after the resurrection of Jesus, when
Thomas begins to hear reports that the man he watched die on a Roman
cross is actually now alive. His friends were locked away in a room, not
unlike a tomb that had been sealed. The barriers the disciples had constructed, though, were no match for the one who could not be held in
check by the barrier between life and death. Still, having not seen this
christological transgression of life's barriers for himself, Thomas is less
than sure. "Unless I see the nail marks in his hands and put my finger
where the nails were, and put my hand into his side, I will not believe,"
he tells his friends (Jn 20:25).

A week later, Thomas gets his wish. "Though the doors were locked,
Jesus came and stood among them and said, 'Peace be with you!' Then
he said to Thomas, 'Put your finger here; see my hands. Reach out your
hand and put it into my side. Stop doubting and believe'" (Jn 20:26-27).

---

[3]Casey Tygrett, *Becoming Curious: A Spiritual Practice of Asking Questions* (Downers Grove, IL:
InterVarsity Press: 2017), 16.
[4]Karl Barth, *Evangelical Theology: An Introduction* (Grand Rapids, MI: Eerdmans, 1963), 121.

As much as I do not want to pause at the height of this story to look at grammar, we cannot leave Jesus' statement unexamined because the words we use to retell this story carry a lot of theological weight. Most English translations of the Bible will assign the word *doubt* where John uses the term *apistos*. Out of the more than twenty times *apistos* is used in the New Testament, this is the only place where it tends to get translated into English as "doubt." There is a word in Greek that more closely means "doubt" as we use it today, but that is not what shows up in this passage.[5] *Apistos* is the negative form of *pistos*, which is often translated "believe." English speakers regularly use this kind of negation when we affix the letter *a* to the beginning of a word to negate its meaning. "Don't be so apathetic," we might say to a friend who is having trouble finding excitement in a particular activity. Really, what we have just done is negate *pathos*, a word we often associate with passion. In another example, an atheist is simply a negated theist. Greek functions the same way in the term John employs here, so that when we read the English word *doubt*, it is more like "disbelief"—the negated form of *belief*. "Do not disbelieve, but believe," is the way we would translate it if that made any sense to everyday English speakers.

The point here is that Jesus does not tell Thomas to stop asking questions, wondering, or pressing issues. It was never his questions that led Thomas away from belief in Jesus. His quest for certainty, however, seems to be a bit more problematic for his belief, and it is on this point that Jesus engages Thomas directly. "Unless I see . . . and touch," Thomas begins. What ultimately provokes Thomas's cry of belief, though, is not some kind of verification but an encounter with Jesus himself. Here we have a culmination of all the times Jesus tells the disciples to believe *in* him. They were never supposed to believe in some kind of empirical proof *about* Jesus. They were, as it turns out, supposed to believe *in him*. Belief, then, is not a matter of holding some facts in mind; it is what happens when we entrust ourselves to the one we encounter, the living Christ,

---

[5]Matthew's Gospel uses *distazō* in passages such as Mt 14:31, when Jesus asks Peter, "Why did you doubt?"

provoking the last words we hear from Thomas: "My Lord and my God!" (Jn 20:28).

I do not know why this exclamation is not Thomas's legacy. I do not know why he is remembered for doubt when his story really concludes with belief. What I do see here, however, is that his declaration of faith comes after a living encounter with the resurrected Christ. His questions uncovered new depths of knowledge, but they could not produce a faith exclamation. Only an encounter with Jesus could do that for him. In other words, Thomas's doubt—his honest questions in search of answers—offered him something profound, but it could not substitute for an encounter with the Word that became flesh. A living encounter with the resurrected Christ was categorically different for him, for it produced a response that his other approaches could not. Neither blind zeal nor pressing examination could elicit what an encounter with Jesus could. Zeal and questioning are a vital part of the theological journey, as we learn from Thomas. But it is only a living encounter with the resurrected Christ that can produce the doxological words of praise that mark the zenith of his theological journey: "My Lord and my God!"

DECONSTRUCTING DOUBT

What exactly do we mean when we say *doubt*? Doubt has a long, complicated, and fascinating history that we cannot fully account for here, but doubt's role in theology will largely depend on what we think it is. Thomas helps us to make a distinction between two kinds of doubt and their role in the theological life. The first kind is what I will call indifferent distrust. The second kind is what I will refer to as committed questioning.

Let us take a closer look at doubt in the way it is most often understood, as *indifferent distrust*. This is the kind of doubt that may not be necessarily antagonistic or oppositional to belief but questions everything without ever having to commit to anything. It is probably a truer account of doubt to the origins of the English word, a linguistic descendant of Latin words such as *dubitare* and *duo*. That first Latin term gives us the word *dubious*, and the second means "two," as in *double*. (The Gospel writers take the time to indicate that Thomas was a twin—a double.) Taken together, our use of the word *doubt* has tended to signify being double-minded or torn between two realities. More than anything, it is an attempt to shield oneself from commitment.

I have a lot of compassion for this kind of doubt because I am the type of person who can see a lot of things from both sides. At times, I envy people who appear to operate out of such single-sided conviction that they do not have to grapple with the complexity of opposing ideas. "Living in the tension" is a phrase that people like me have most likely invented to get by in a complex world.

Let me be clear, though: the world is a complex place, and truth is rarely served by simplifying things for the sake of being able to take a position. Most of the time, something is not *all* good or *all* bad. There is, then, a latent temptation to "live in the tension" so that we do not have to commit to anything. Commitment comes with its own trouble, and whether it is our positions on moral issues, theological alignments, or community associations, we late modern people are quite adept at making our way through life without having to make many commitments.

Given so much of what we have seen, how could it be otherwise? The curtain has been pulled back on organizations, institutions, churches, political parties, and people who have long presented a publicly pristine veneer, now exposing a complex swirl of motivations and commitments. Among those people and organizations we thought to be singly devoted to goodness, saintly self-sacrifice and unsightly sins share space. Many of us have come to discover that committing to people and places makes it nearly impossible to filter out the toxic contaminants from the life-giving nutrients in the soil that nourished our growth. The fruit of distrust flourishes in polluted fields. So, when the search for unadulterated soil returns void, we are more comfortable pulling up our roots altogether, dropping into relationships with institutions or people occasionally, living largely as voyeurs but rarely allowing anything to truly get ahold of us.

It is hard to blame anyone for adopting this form of doubt when such disorienting discoveries are made. My examination here is not at all intended to make this approach to doubt shameful, but we do need to take an honest account of what kinds of pathways open to us methodologically in the work of theology. If doubt is continual uprootedness, it likely will not be able to advance much beyond mere suspicion. In this mode, "Doubt only means swaying and staggering between Yes and No," Barth writes. "It is only an uncertainty, although such uncertainty can be much worse than negation itself."[6] Of course, Barth does not fear negation as a set of ideas that are somehow against God. Negation, for him, is no set of atheistic proofs for the nonexistence of God. Rather, the swaying between yes and no is the kind of thing that is worse. It cannot rise to be able to negate something because it sways back the other direction as soon as it tries. In other words, negation takes commitment at some level, and the kind of doubt that resists commitment wholesale does not have the capacity to negate much at all, be it ideas of God's existence or the unfaithfulness we find in fallen institutions.

During my second or third year of theological study, I bumped up against this kind of swaying indifference. While I cannot recall the finer points of our discussion in the class that day, I do remember a pair of my colleagues who were seemingly blown into our class by the winds of indifferent distrust. They were interesting and esteemed members of the student body, probably because they had learned to live under the mystique of "maybe." As the rest of the class would be chewing on some thought-provoking issue, one of them would inevitably raise their hand and inject, "Well, I guess that would work . . . if you believed in God." I am still not sure whether this was meant to shock a room full of earnest theology majors or whether it was something closer to a genuine question. What it did, however, was provide the duo of disillusionment cover from having to make any kind of commitment to any theological position or take a single step in any given direction. In short, it stalled out any kind of theological exploration.

[6]Barth, *Evangelical Theology*, 124.

These young questioners were, of course, correct about some form of belief in God being necessary to have a coherent conversation about things such as divine love or God's activity in the world. For them, however, this necessary commitment was not one they made, and it tended to shut down the conversation. After several weeks of their mysterious theological bomb-dropping, the methodological issue dawned on me: we were not going to get very far if even the most basic commitments of theology were not made. "I understand that you may not believe in God," I said to them one afternoon, "but in order for us to explore any of the rest of this, we are going to need to proceed as if we do." It probably was not an artful thing to say, and I hope it left room for genuine care and expression, but at that moment, I wished they had either joined the conversation or espoused a full-blown atheism. Operating from indifference was stopping the conversation from going anywhere.

While not every theological approach may need to be held for a lifetime, there are certain commitments that are necessary to evaluate those approaches. I am grateful that some of the theological commitments I made when I was twenty no longer hold me, but without them I would not have been able to truly evaluate where they would take me. For at least some time, I had to walk the pathway and then evaluate whether it was taking me closer to a faithful commitment to the way of truth in Jesus Christ.

Employing doubt that operates as across-the-board indifference, uprooting us from commitments at large, runs the risk of buffering us from commitments in general or allowing genuine exploration. When this happens, we do uncommitted theology as uncommitted people, and our brand of theology can become little more than voyeuristic spectating, as if we were watching a parade go by while offering commentary about the quality of the entries.

Somehow, I was raised in California without ever attending the Rose Parade. Technically, I have gone once to look at the floats after the parade had ended, so maybe that counts. That visit, however, taught me to evaluate the floats in the Rose Parade differently from while sitting in my house and watching the parade on TV every New Year's Day. Stepping up to see the floats closely opens a level of appreciation for the hours of painstaking work that goes into creating each one. Not only are every one of these rolling works of art completely unique, but they are made from biological material. Flowers, seeds, nuts, twigs—all of it is organic. Standing beside the floats, you can begin to picture volunteers in hangar-sized storage spaces, committed to working through the cold temperatures and short days to make sure every detail is perfect.

I realized then that I needed to change my approach to watching the Rose Parade. Without the commitment to show up and deal with eight hundred thousand almond blossoms and glue, how could I sit in the relative comfort of a folding chair from the sidewalk and pronounce my evaluation of these floats? That morning, I realized that the commitment of the float makers was always going to allow them an insight I would never have as a spectator, looking on from the side of the parade route.

Commitment distinguishes between the kind of doubt we have just discussed and the kind that Thomas demonstrates. From his "Let us also go, that we may die with him," to his "My Lord and my God!" Thomas demonstrates the kind of commitment to a living person that makes committed questioning possible. His commitment to Jesus is what allows his questions to drive him to deeper knowledge of a person he cannot entirely wrap his mind around. Commitment is necessary, at some level, to being able to ask questions that allow you to explore in earnest, even if you cannot be sure where all that commitment will ultimately take you.

That kind of commitment, of course, reminds me of marriage. In October 2005, I found myself standing at an altar in the company of friends and family, flanked by my pastor. A young woman wearing white appeared at the back of the church, and I waited for the moment that others had described to me, when time would freeze and all would be right with the universe. For someone with my intellectual wiring, it was more like being taken up in a snowstorm of questions, because this was a commitment that was larger than what I could imagine. Where would we live five years from now? What would happen if one of us got sick? Were we going to be able to string together enough of an income to pay the bills? What if she did something I did not agree with? Was she going to hurt me? Even if I were somehow able to get answers to those kinds of questions (and I most certainly could not), this commitment was larger still than even those answers. As much as I thought about it, I could not gain certainty about what our future would look like or where exactly this commitment would take me, but I knew I was ready to commit to this *person*. Without commitment to this living, mysterious person, I was not going to know her more. Without committing on some level, I would never be able to discover the answers to the questions I had. Commitment was opening the capacity for knowledge in a way that a disinterested familiarity never could. I was going to commit to someone who would surprise me, someone who would cause me pain and bring delight. "You are this whole other person," I still say to her today, which is my way of marveling at the fact that I have pledged my fidelity to someone I know better than anyone else on the planet and who is still a mystery to me.

In some way, all human relationships work like this. Friendships, parent-child relationships, employment agreements—all of these require some commitment to be able to really know the truth about what they are. As many questions as I might ask about what a particular job will be like, I will never know it in depth until I sign the paperwork and show up for work.

Methodologically, we could try to do theology without commitment. We could ask lots of questions, inquire about biblical sources, and use modern approaches to try to peel back the layers of religious experience, but this would be a lot like trying to get to know what a friendship would be like by interviewing potential companions. It will give you some information about them, but there is a good chance you will never know what it is like to be friends with them until you give yourself to it.

Because Christian theology will always involve the study of the God who became flesh and made his dwelling among us, the God who dwells with us still in the person of the Holy Spirit, there will always need to be some kind of commitment necessary to know this one who has known us. It is the kind of commitment that cannot be produced by examining or verifying from the outside. To consider it in light of the locked upper room in John 20, Thomas does not come to belief through examining Jesus' wounds, even though that is his first impulse, and Jesus invites him to do so. No, Thomas's proclamation of belief is one of commitment, throwing himself into living relationship first. The wounds in Jesus' body will be far more than proof of concept for Thomas. They now become definitive for who he is, for in committing himself to Jesus, he is truly believing *in* Jesus, and to believe in a God-man resurrected with wounds in his flesh is to give yourself to a future reality where we may be resurrected with wounds of our own.

COMMITMENT AND QUESTIONING

The kind of doubt we see in Thomas is the kind that leads with commitment, risky as it is. His knowledge is no buffered, disinterested knowledge, and this is what leads him to know in ways that idea proofs cannot produce. More than anything, this commitment to a living, wounded, resurrected person—mysterious and potentially perilous as he is to Thomas—will be what allows him to bring his honest questions and know Jesus more.

We might say that Thomas's kind of doubt is something like Socrates (with a caveat). Socrates, Plato's teacher and the "gadfly of Athens" who lived four hundred years before Jesus, was known for asking honest questions. Plato's writings offer a vision of Socrates who wanted to know something in the depths of its parts. He was not going to be satisfied with pat or simple answers, primarily because those answers were not going to open the depths of truth he craved. Socrates was known for taking an idea such as justice or piety and dissecting it until he could see it from all its angles. His philosopher's scalpel would cut away anything that stood in the way of knowing something truthfully. Nothing could be taken at face value. So, everything and everyone was up for rigorous questioning in Athens. When Socrates caught even the slightest whiff of confusion or contradiction in something one of Athens's leaders might say, he went to work, carving up the idea with his questions, refusing to let the person leave until they had examined the statement from every angle. No wonder they were quick to put him to death.

Thomas's questioning, it seems to me, functions a lot like Socratic doubt. He is not the type of person to let a statement such as "You know the way to the place where I am going" get by at face value. His Socratic doubt surfaces quickly: "No we don't! How could we? You haven't told us where you're going. I want to know more." Yes, he may be a bit frustrated, but his frustration is driven by a commitment to know more, and this is where we can distinguish the first kind of doubt from the second.

The caveat, of course, is that while Socrates wanted to know the truth of *ideas* inside and out, Thomas was under no impression that Jesus was an idea. Jesus is a person—divine and human—who must be known as such. When Christian theologians seek to know truth, then, they are not merely interrogating ideas but are coming to know the one who says to Thomas, "I am the way, *and the truth*, and the life." In Christian theology, truth is a person, and commitment to him opens a way of knowing that allows us to ask honest questions.

Ideas, concepts, or propositions rarely surprise us the way a living person can. We can trust a concept to remain the same from the time we come to know it. The concept that two of something and two more of something will make four somethings is a stable concept that is not likely to surprise us any time soon. It might have been a realization when we first learned it, but once we mastered the concept, it could be trusted to not surprise us anymore.

Thomas's trouble is that he is not looking at a concept. He is looking at a living, crucified, resurrected person. His commitment is pledged to a resurrected man who may end up surprising him—the thrill of theology! For those who pledge their commitment to the resurrected Christ, there is always the possibility of being surprised. As in discipleship, doing theology after Jesus is giving yourself first and allowing intellectual discovery to flow from the methods that emerge from committing yourself to a crucified, resurrected revelation of God. Pledging commitment to a person also opens the possibility of bringing honest questions without forsaking the commitment.

The primary commitment a theologian makes to be able to ask honest questions is to God, embodied in the person of Jesus Christ. That commitment opens the thrilling capacity for us to ask questions, a quest to know the living God in new depth and wonder. The simple reality is that doing theology will require commitment from us before we understand all of it, and in this sense it is an act of love for a living God. It never was the answers to questions that were going to get Thomas into the flow of theology. It was his commitment to the living Christ.

Making this commitment allows us to honestly question the other commitments in our lives. Bringing honest questions to the church, for example, will serve it well when our commitment is to Christ, the church's head (Col 1:18). This is the kind of commitment that can allow theologians to be committed to the church's faithfulness even when the church has been unfaithful. Theologians are not critics on the side of the parade route, idly critiquing the failings of an institution in a posture of disinterest. Ours is a call to call the church to holiness, which first calls for a commitment to the one who gives the church its life.

When theologians bring honest questions to the church, then, they are questions of commitment. When theologians bring critiques, they are not from the sidelines, as if we were disinterested in the community God has called to bear witness to the gospel. The questions we bring are honest to God, calling the church into faithful alignment with the crucified and resurrected Jesus Christ.

We should not shy away from it: issuing critiques may earn us wounds in our flesh. When theologians issue critiques without commitment, the wounds we suffer may be enough to send us looking for another line of work. But if commitment is first to the crucified and resurrected Christ, not only will the critiques we issue flow from our commitment to Christ, but our wounds, too, will shine forth with the glory of a crucified body participating in the hope of resurrection. Uncommitted questioning results only in marks from a battle we may have fled because the cost was not worth the gain; wounds shot through with glory begin with Thomas's virtue of commitment: "My Lord and my God!"

DOUBTING CERTAINTY

We cannot leave Thomas before examining further his need for proof, especially in light of modern theological method. "Unless I see the nail marks in his hands," Thomas tells his friends, "and put my finger where the nails were, and put my hand into his side, I will not believe" (Jn 20:25). At first glance, this may appear to be a need for the certainty of empirical proof. What we cannot miss, though, is that Thomas never actually touches Jesus. Rather, his cry of commitment to Jesus is something beyond what empiricism can deliver.

Of course, much theology in the past three centuries has operated along the lines of providing empirical proof for theology's claims. Scientific materialism's methods went to work on the imagination of theologians, shaping theology to produce proofs that could satisfy those who had come to root truth on something that was verifiable—knowledge we could hold. In the field of theology itself, methods such as *historical criticism* sought to apply empirical tools to the study of ancient texts so that modern readers could separate out the faith claims embedded in the text from the cold, hard, historical facts. Our purpose here is not to level a wholesale critique of these kinds of methods. Indeed, Jesus does not reject Thomas's request to see and touch, and even invites him to do just that, so a wholesale rejection of empirical verification is not consistent with what we see in Thomas's encounter with the resurrected Christ. Rather, it is to point out that when it comes to doubt, methods designed to deliver certainty reduce the need for commitment, in turn reducing a capacity to bring honest questions. That is, a method aimed at erasing doubt in the name of certainty may bypass the risks of commitment, but it also short-circuits the honest questions that open truth to us anew.

"Unless I see and touch . . ." Thomas says. Quickly, however, this quest for certainty is eclipsed by an encounter with the living person of Jesus.

Thomas's conviction that he needs to have the kind of knowledge that he can take hold of and touch gives way to knowledge afforded by knowing the person who is standing before him.

John does not tell us any more about Thomas's conversations with Jesus beyond his proclamation of faith. I would like to think, however, that rather than this closing the chapter on Thomas, it opens a wide array of theological discovery. I would also like to think that Thomas did not stop asking questions, because his cry of commitment to the risen Christ is a new beginning point for honest questions. Thomas's testimony is that commitment opens a world of theological knowledge that certainty alone cannot deliver.

In 1602, the famous painter Caravaggio offered up his rendition of Thomas's encounter with the risen Christ. In his arresting style that invites the viewer to take a place as a participant in the scene, Caravaggio depicts Thomas with a dirty finger outstretched, penetrating the wound in Jesus' side. Jesus has Thomas by the wrist and is guiding the doubting disciple to place his hand into the Savior's side. The whole event is punctuated by the expression Thomas wears, highlighting not only the painter's mastery of depicting human emotion but also Thomas's complex combination of wonder, fear, and disbelief melting into belief.

For a host of theological reasons we do not have time to explore here, I love this painting. The trouble is, John never tells us that this scene happened. As far as we know from the biblical story, Thomas does not ever take Jesus up on his invitation to place his hand into the wounds he bears. As much as I love Jesus' hand guiding Thomas into a faith-forming encounter with his resurrected flesh, I love even more what John tells us about this encounter: Thomas does not take hold of Jesus. It is a theme John wants us to see. "Do not hold on to me," he recounts Jesus saying to Mary when she first encountered him in the garden, just before the scene with Thomas unfolds (Jn 20:17). Relinquishing the need to take hold of Jesus reminds us that we are not taking hold of knowledge to bring it under our control, to "have" it. Mary taking hold and Thomas reaching out to touch risk making the resurrection a proof beyond doubt.

In these divine encounters, they are not going to prove an idea but encounter a person.

All of Thomas's demands to see and touch dissipate when he encounters the Word in resurrected flesh. Taking hold indicates a methodological disaster, that theology is no longer a logic of wonders but something to be proven beyond the shadow of a doubt. When Christian theology must be proven at all costs, we are more likely seeking control than wonder. If Jesus were a truth that could be grasped and held by Thomas, he would not be a truth worth committing to. Thomas teaches us to plunge into commitment, risking ourselves on the kind of truth that can only be found when we surrender into a mystery.

Thomas teaches us that climbing aboard our doubt as if it were a vehicle headed into pure certainty is not going to silence our questioning. Uncertainty is not the enemy of theology. Theology is "a quest for truth . . . that is never completed."[7] It can, however, produce a commitment to something we cannot hold on to, something that wondrously eludes our grasp, even as it calls us deeper into its beauty. It is precisely because Jesus cannot be laid hold of that he can be exclaimed as Thomas's Lord and God.

In Thomas's story, there is uncomfortable truth and incomparable freedom for those who doubt. Namely, the uncomfortable truth is that Jesus is not a concept to be mastered. The freedom, too, is that he is not a concept to be deciphered but a living Lord to be followed. Theology simply does not work along the lines of concepts that we can hold in our hand and take under our control. Christian theology is always the logic of wonders because it is what happens in the encounter with a living God who is free and has a long history of surprising us. If our doubts are aimed at laying hold of certainty, whatever we take hold of will most likely be something other than theological knowledge. Jesus—the living one—*is* the way, and the truth, and the life, and whatever doubt we use to know this living and resurrected Christ, it cannot take him in hand. The

---

[7]Barth, *Evangelical Theology*, 121.

theological quest does not end in the certainty of being able to take concepts into our hand, because its aim is more rightly commitment to a living and resurrected Christ. Thus, Thomas does not overcome his doubts with a cry of, "My rightness and my certainty!" but "My Lord and my God!"

PRAYER

Our Lord and our God,
We confess that we do not always know where you are going
    or where you are taking us.
Give us the commitment, we ask, to follow you anyway.
Free us from the guilt we may feel for the questions we ask.
    Make them be for us a companion
On the journey of knowing you more.
By your gracious invitation, teach us to press more deeply into the
    mysteries of your goodness.
Open our eyes, we ask, to a vision of who you are, that we might be
    drawn to you.
Remind us that you stand open, inviting us to know you more.
May your goodness call us out of indifference; may it summon us
    to ask more of who you are,
That we might give you praise,
Now and forever,
Amen.

QUESTIONS FOR DISCUSSION OR REFLECTION

1. Have you ever been made to feel that your questions were dangerous? How does Thomas's story bring you encouragement in your own journey of faith?

2. Consider where you might fall if you were to locate yourself along Thomas's timeline. Are you at a point of zeal, committed questioning, needing certainty, or in awe of a living encounter? How might this be shaping the kind of theological work you are doing?

3. How would you describe the difference between committed questioning and indifferent distrust, and what they produce? What are your experiences with each?

4. Where do you fall on the spectrum between requiring certainty and accepting uncertainty? Is this where you want to be? How have you arrived where you are, and how will this shape your work as a theologian?

CHAPTER ELEVEN

Martha and Mary

ON GRIEVING

FOR BETTER OR WORSE, theology tends to be done around grief, loss, and trauma. As we are sitting in the pain of shattered dreams, theological questions become more potent as we grasp for meaning or solace. Sometimes in that search, we reach for whatever we can get ahold of. Those who work around grief as theological practitioners know this well, which is why they of all people might hesitate to invite others into times of grief. "I've heard people say too many foolish things in times like these," a friend of mine told me as he lay in a hospital bed, measuring the advice of medical professionals to begin hospice care. His decades of pastoral ministry were filled with examples of hospital bedside theology done by well-meaning people who were simply trying to make sense of the situation under a cloud of grief. "We can let people know I'm here when the time is right," he said.

Still, that afternoon, we chewed on the things of God. We partook of the Communion elements I brought along and blessed at his bedside. We talked about whether certain kinds of burial practices align well with our confession that our bodies are created good by God and will be resurrected one day. Grief simply has a way of provoking theological questions and theological work. Situations like my friend's, who preferred to be in a hospital alone rather than invite those who might try their hand at theology in a moment of sadness, may invite questions of whether grief is a good companion to theology. Enough troubling theology has been done in moments of sadness that we could be forgiven for dismissing or resisting the notion that grief should be a companion in the theological life.

There is, however, no avoiding grief, at least not for the entirety of a human lifetime. Further still, the collected wisdom of our theological ancestors testifies to God's mysterious presence in the midst of grief. "Even the darkness will not be dark to you," the psalmist prays, having previously confessed that there is nowhere he can go where God's presence will not meet him (Ps 139:12). The "But I trust in your unfailing love" of Psalm 13 lyrically penetrates the heart of grief, meeting the cries of one who demands an answer from God when he feels abandoned with a reminder of divine presence we can find in the darkness (Ps 13:5). Could these kinds of meetings open us to know God in ways inaccessible to us on the easy days? Is there a type of theological virtue to be found as we traverse the field of grief? A certain reading of Martha and Mary's story of sorrow reveals a way—a method, even—of knowing something of God in the midst of grief, and we will turn to their story shortly.

Were it not for John's inclusion of their story in his Gospel, I would likely have turned away from grief as a means of theological discovery, primarily because of the way it is so often sloppily portrayed as a blessing in disguise. The causes of human suffering are too varied and complex for us to cozy up to grief as a kindly and sage teacher, and it is too tempting to comfort ourselves by belittling the suffering of a friend by pointing out everything they are learning. There is no lesson grief can teach us that makes the loss worth the lesson. No, we must let grief be grief. Grief is a special kind of pain. It is at once an unholy trinity of goodness being unraveled in front of us, the familiar stability of our life being shaken from its moorings, and a shaky search for a path forward in a dark forest on a moonless night.

Given this, what place does grief have in the theological life? As a nearly universal reality of the human experience, grief may not be a kind teacher, but it is not lost to God. In fact, we may run the risk of getting something really wrong in our theological work if we do not allow grief to enter our consideration. Of course, the way we encounter and engage grief will depend on what kind of God we think we are dealing with. It is striking how often a person's response to grief looks so much like the image of God they carry with them so deeply in their theological imagination that it has seeped into their bones. But we are not talking about that here because I am not attempting to offer a theology of grief, precisely, and besides, there are many other books on these topics. In this journey, we are on our way to Bethany, a village not far from Jerusalem, where we will sit with Martha and Mary, two sisters who encounter God's presence while in the throes of grief. If we listen carefully, these sisters of sorrow have something to teach us about coming to a deeper understanding of divine character and activity as they are working through the death of their brother, Lazarus. In their witness, we find a type of theological virtue that can only come to us through our grappling with grief, precisely because we have met God there, in the midst of sorrow.

COME AND SEE

We meet Martha and Mary in John 11. Luke tells us a story about these sisters as well, but John alone gives us the story of their grief over Lazarus. Lazarus, as we see in John's account, is sick and dying, and these sisters send word to Jesus, who is about a day's journey from their hometown of Bethany. John weaves some of his favorite theological themes into the conversation Jesus has with his disciples prior to going to help Lazarus. Belief, light, dark, and seeing are all part of the conversation, foreshadowing the events that will unfold when Jesus finally makes his way to Bethany and raises Lazarus from the dead.

Part of this story's richness is its capacity to demonstrate each of the sisters' grief responses. Like the rest of us, they each handle grief differently, especially in relationship to God. Like many other types of differences, our instinct may be to ask which is preferable or superior. I raise that explicitly to suggest that we resist the impulse to compare the sisters in search of a superior grief response, as is often done with this story. My reading of John 11 is not as much about which sister's response is better as it is about Jesus' *movement* toward the heart of grief. A question resides under the surface of this story: Does our theological method allow us to meet and know God in grief?

When the story opens, we find Jesus a couple of miles from Bethany. It is not too far for a day trip, but the distance between Jesus and the one he loves who is sick is highlighted by the fact that Jesus stays where he is, rather than making the journey (Jn 11:6). Before he enters Bethany, Martha meets him, identifying him in kinetic terms as "the Messiah, the Son of God, who is *to come into* the world" (Jn 11:27). Mary picks up there with Jesus as he is ushered closer and closer to the cause of their pain. Jesus' journey of movement reaches its heartrending conclusion as he breaks down in tears as he draws near to Lazarus's tomb, prompting not only the onlooking crowd to give witness to Jesus' love for Lazarus but also the reader to see that his movement has reached its sorrowful destination (Jn 11:36). Overall, John 11 testifies to a God who moves closer to the source of our pain, moved by love for the one who has died and those who are grieving. Together, Martha and Mary usher Jesus closer to the heart of their sorrow, a method in which we may find theological virtue.

Taking the sisters in the order of their encounter with Jesus, Martha is the one who proactively leaves her home, apparently unwilling to wait until Jesus makes his way to Bethany. Like the countless who have endured the loss of a loved one, Martha is undoubtedly being thrust into a world she does not want, where her brother is no longer alive, and she is forced to endure "the collapse of the world of stories she had lived inside."[1]

"If you had been here," she pointedly says to Jesus, "my brother would not have died" (Jn 11:21). There is respectable audacity in her statement, which stops just short of being an accusatory question: "Where have you been?" Her statement is followed by another: "But I know that even now God will give you whatever you ask" (Jn 11:22). If the boldness of her first

---

[1]Greg Garrett, *Stories from the Edge: A Theology of Grief* (Louisville, KY: Westminster John Knox, 2008), x.

statement generates respect, certainly this second statement, forged in the fires of faith, should as well. Martha seems quite assured that had Jesus been present, Lazarus would not have died, but that this can be overlooked because Jesus can do something about it now.

This statement and the one that will follow begin with Martha's declarative "I know." At least as John presents her in this story, she is a woman who leads with what she knows. Even speaking to Jesus, she seems quite assured of what he can do. "I know he will rise again in the resurrection at the last day," she says of her deceased brother (Jn 11:24). Finally, her declarative assurance reaches its height in her response to Jesus when he asks her whether she affirms that those who believe in him will find life. "Yes, Lord," she replies, "I believe that you are the Messiah, the Son of God, who is to come into the world" (Jn 11:27). Eleven chapters into John's Gospel, even the casual reader knows that belief is the height of what Jesus is after in John's account. This, then, is no small statement on Martha's part. Everything we have come to expect that is right and good is found in her. She is one who has her beliefs in order.

Looking more carefully at Martha's interaction with Jesus, let us remember that belief is the high standard of relationship to Christ, at least as John presents it. "Search the Hebrew Bible for the word *belief* and it shows up rarely in this meaning—belief in God," Jennifer Michael Hecht points out. "Daniel got out of the lion's den because he believed in his God, and here and there people are said to not believe what a given prophet has said, but that's it. Then when Jesus appears, the word *believe* blooms like a patch of poppies in a great green field. Suddenly, it is the heart of the matter."[2] For John, perhaps even more than any of the Synoptic Gospel writers, this is certainly the case, and Martha is a paragon of one of John's highest theological virtues. If Jesus is gladdened that this situation has unfolded "so that you may believe," she is a beacon of light in the darkness, especially for the disciples who have accompanied Jesus to Bethany (Jn 11:15). Drawing from her own tradition's history of lament,

---

[2]Jennifer Michael Hecht, *Doubt: A History* (San Francisco: HarperOne, 2004), 175-76.

Martha's trusting confession welcomes Jesus' redemptive presence. Though a mixture of anger and sadness—grief's unmistakably unique ingredients—her response echoes the psalmist: "But I trust."

From everything John tells us, Jesus does not seem to have any trouble with Martha's affirmations of belief. He uses the opportunity to expand her understanding, but nowhere do we see that her beliefs are a problem for what Jesus has come to do. What we do see, however, is that this is a conversation that takes place on the outskirts of grief's center, and Jesus did not come to stop there. In a sense, his conversation with Martha is like a porch where the two pause before entering the house. It is a place where Jesus is welcomed and the door is opened to take another step. Her confession is not opposed to the work Jesus has come to do, but importantly, it is also not the entirety of his work. We could say it another way: Martha is rightly assured that Jesus is "the Messiah, the Son of God, who is to come into the world," a clear support of the theological case John has set out to make about Jesus from the opening of his Gospel (Jn 11:27). What remains unclear is whether Martha sees Jesus coming into *her* world.

Our beliefs in and confessions of who Jesus is and his ability to do the work are not problematic for the work of theology, especially as they relate to grief. Certainly, we do well to confess what is true about God's redemptive work in and among a fallen world, plagued by death, disease, and injustice. Yet, our beliefs are not the heart of the theological life: God's life and work is. Grief has a special way of reminding us of this. When the darkness of death and destruction surrounds, we do well to confess our belief in the God who has moved into our fallen world—and then we do well to watch God work, that we might have more to confess. We can say a lot that is technically orthodox about God, but such confession takes on a new depth and dimension when God's activity engages the very heart of the death and injustice that cause our grief. Correct concepts are no enemy to theology, but they do not constitute the entirety of theology. When our desire to uphold and maintain our concepts about God become more central to theology than God's actual work in the world, we can be sure that something is amiss in our method, and virtue tilts toward vice.

To be clear, Martha's confession is good and right, and Jesus wants to fill out her confession in real, embodied ways. Correct concepts will not raise her dead brother, but Jesus will. It is right that she confesses her belief "in the resurrection at the last day" (Jn 11:24), but Jesus takes the next step: "*I am the resurrection and the life*" (Jn 11:25, emphasis added). The good news, then, is that when we may be tempted to mistake our ideas and concepts for the whole of our theology, the work of God goes on making the world new, giving us something more to confess and stirring our praise anew. Grief has a special way of highlighting this reality, as it often shines a spotlight on those places that are causing the most pain, the places where God's activity tends to be at work.

The joyful virtue of theology is confessing what God has done and is doing. Often we theologians are trained to find the best way of doing so that we possibly can. We carefully select our words in prayerful hope that what we are saying is faithful to God and God's activity. Robert Jenson's delightful axiom rings true: "Theology is thinking what to say to be saying the gospel."[3] Of course, this will take into account the way one concept relates to another, so that what we say about the Holy Spirit in the work of *pneumatology*, for example, is logically related to, say, *ecclesiology*, which is the study of the church. Theologians are called to offer faithful concepts communicated in truthful words, and yet, making the work of theology entirely about our words and concepts risks losing sight of the very reality we set out to proclaim.

Here is where it is important to name that Martha and Mary are not opposed to each other. Martha's affirmation of belief is not set against Mary's own action here, in the same way that affirming belief in God is not opposed to bearing witness to God's activity, especially in the midst of death and grief. In holding the sisters together, rather than comparing them to each other, we see the movement of Jesus into the heart of their

---

[3]Robert Jenson, *Systematic Theology*, vol. 1, *The Triune God* (Oxford: Oxford University Press, 1997), 32.

collective grief. Martha's affirmation of belief in Jesus welcomes him to the situation; Mary's invitation to Jesus continues what began on the porch into the heart of the matter. Meeting Jesus where her sister left him, Mary begins exactly how her sister had: "Lord, if you had been here, my brother would not have died" (Jn 11:32). Then, silence.

For Mary, there are no assertive proclamations about belief. There are only tears. Mary's tears, apparently, are enough to do something in Jesus. Being "deeply moved in spirit and troubled" is an accurate, if tepid, translation of John's words (*enebrimēsato, etaraxen*) for Jesus' response to Mary's sorrow (Jn 11:33). The words John chose to relay Jesus' reaction signal empathy, but they are flavored with fury. They are words that help us catch a glimpse of just what kind of God sits with us in our grief. If we do not get this, we do not get God. Death and the tears it causes are apparently what makes Jesus angry enough to shed a few of his own. "Where have you laid him?" Jesus asks, signaling that his journey into the center of grief is taking one last step forward. "Come and see," she invites (Jn 11:34).

"Come and see" is a common refrain in John's Gospel. Sprinkled throughout the opening chapters in particular, this invitational phrase functions not only as a testimony to those in the story seeing Jesus but also as a summons to the reader to do the same. This time is different, though, because it is the only time we see this as an invitation issued *to* Jesus. What awaits Jesus if he accepts it? Grief.

Of all the things the sisters could have invited Jesus to come and see, why grief? Why *their* grief? After all, Jesus has only asked where they have laid Lazarus's body, and they could have answered him with some factual answer: "We put him in the tomb over there." But their response is more proactive than that. They want to take Jesus into the heart of the sorrowful matter, and here a Mary-informed vision of doing theology in grief begins to come into view. She believes in what he is there to do among the painful realities of life that cause her grief. She ushers Jesus toward the heart of her grief, and there she will witness the work God does in the midst of the world's deepest pain.

LAMENT IN THE WORK OF THEOLOGY

For Mary and her sister Martha, though, their invitation to Jesus is part of a deeper, richer grief practice they had known since they were children. "Come and see, Lord" is not only a pragmatic response to Jesus' question or a touchpoint for one of John's favorite theological themes—it is also lament. Whether it is our collective tendency to avoid pain and sorrow or a societal expectation that most of human life should be happy, lament has faded into the background of the contemporary picture of grief. Lament is no quick checkpoint on our way to healing. It is, rather, the willingness to sit down right there in the sorrow and refuse to move until you have said every last thing you need to say. It is the arena of complaint, where you are given permission to ask your honest questions and voice your charges against every injustice, every pain-causing problem, and even God himself. Certainly, this is no way to do the work of theology in the polite company of those who have seemed to master the art of self-possession, and that, perhaps, is precisely the problem.

Martha and Mary teach us something of what theological discoveries we might find in lament. Not only are these women not afraid of lament, but the presence of Jewish mourners from Jerusalem at their brother's funeral signals that they are actively using this ancient practice of grief. When the nearby holy city had been laid waste, their own ancestors envisioned Jerusalem itself in feminine form, crying out to be seen, heard, and comforted in a time of sorrow. "Zion stretches out her hands," the narrator of Lamentations says, "but there is no one to comfort her" (Lam 1:17). When she herself is given voice, the echo sounds even more like the cries we hear from Martha and Mary. "This is why I weep and my eyes overflow with tears," she says. "No one is near to comfort me, no one to restore my spirit" (Lam 1:16). Confronted with the sorrow of a disaster that has ripped away life as she had known it, the weeping Daughter Zion of Lamentations is immediately met with another difficulty: no one is there to bring her comfort. Sitting in the rubble of a life upended, she longs for the solace of a comforter who apparently is nowhere to be found. Of this plaintive passage, Kathleen O'Conner writes,

"The comforter in Lamentations does more than offer gestures and words—he or she is an elusive poetic figure whose *absence* emphasizes Zion's suffering isolation."[4] As the Bethany sisters both put it, "If you had been here . . ."

Even if it is not an arm around the shoulder, the least Daughter Zion hopes for is someone to see her in her grief. "Look, LORD, on my affliction," she begs. "Look, LORD, and consider, for I am despised" (Lam 1:9, 11). Maybe these were the only kinds of words that would come to the sisters' mind when their own grief overflowed: "Come and see, Lord" (Jn 11:34). Then, "Jesus wept" (Jn 11:35). Not only does Jesus give witness to the pain that Martha and Mary are enduring, but he enters into it, even to the point that he is deeply moved in his spirit. The absence of a comforter for Jerusalem is met by Jesus' movement into the heart of their sorrow. The cries of the sisters' great-grandmother in grief, still true in its own right, take on new depths as Jesus goes beyond comforting their spirits but takes their grief into his own spirit. For these sisters, Jesus is the comforter who finally showed up. He is the presence of the God who sees them in their pain, has come near, and weeps with them.

Nicholas Wolterstorff's words in his *Lament for a Son* are painfully appropriate. There, out of the deep shadow of his twenty-five-year-old son's death, these words emerge:

> But please: Don't say it's not really so bad. Because it is. Death is awful, demonic. If you think your task as comforter is to tell me that really, all things considered, it's not so bad, you do not sit with me in my grief but place yourself off in the distance away from me. Over there, you are of no help. What I need to hear from you is that you recognize how painful it is. I need to hear from you that you are with me in my desperation. To comfort me, you have to come close.[5]

[4]Kathleen M. O'Conner, *Lamentations and the Tears of the World* (Maryknoll, NY: Orbis Books, 2002), 97, emphasis added.
[5]Nicholas Wolterstorff, *Lament for a Son* (Grand Rapids, MI: Eerdmans, 1987), 34. Quoted in Stanley Hauerwas, *God, Medicine and Suffering* (Grand Rapids, MI: Eerdmans, 1990), 151; O'Conner, *Lamentations and the Tears*, 101; Diane Leclerc and Brent Peterson, *The Back Side of the Cross* (Eugene, OR: Wipf & Stock, 2022), 197.

Mary's impulse to lament, woven into her consciousness from the time of her childhood, reminds us that the kind of theology done through "groanings too deep for words" can offer a glimpse of the God who does not remain at a distance but moves to the heart of her sorrow and is *with* her in her grief (Rom 8:26 NRSVUE). Grief goes where reason alone cannot. Rather than buffer grief with belief, Mary *enacts* grief as a means of belief in God, inviting Jesus to draw near and weep with her. The tears of Christ, I suspect, fall where his followers invite him into places that have been left for dead. They are tears evoked by a mixture of sorrow and gratitude, where the Creator's heart breaks open and re-creation breaks forth.

But there is more theological discovery here: the God who weeps. The Word in flesh, revealed through sobs. Yes, Jesus is joining Martha and Mary in their grief, a profound theological insight in itself, but he is also grieving himself. His tears are his. If we resist grief's role in our theological method, we may be tempted to treat Jesus' tears as one who stands objectively outside sorrow. Our approach could be to *solve* Jesus' tears in ways that attempt to explain how the one true God could cry in an attempt to resolve a tension between the concept of God we hold and the tears we see on Jesus' face. In other words, in our desire to not get our ideas of an all-powerful God wrong, we may be tempted to go to work explaining away Jesus' own sorrow and anger. Allowing grief a space in our theological method, however, opens the capacity for us to realize that we may get God wrong if we do not incorporate Jesus' tears into our understanding of God. When we enact grief—when we allow it into our method and ask what we might discover about God in it—we may find a God we would not expect, "full of grace and truth" with tears gloriously staining his face (Jn 1:14).

Of course, Jesus does not only weep with them. Taking steps into the heart of sorrow, he also speaks a redemptive word of freedom into Lazarus's tomb, and the dead man comes to life. Jesus goes to work on changing the situation in concrete terms. He bears witness to grief, he is moved to hot, angry tears, and he does something about the problem.

In looking to Martha and Mary, we see that tapping into their people's tradition of lament allowed them to get honest with Jesus in an act of theological courage. They were not afraid to name that he was not there when Lazarus died. They did not shy away from telling Jesus that things could have been different if he had adjusted his travel plans. They voiced their twin complaints about his absence, which became points where Jesus moved deeper into the situation, ultimately bringing about some concrete change. In the testimony to these sisters' theological work, their grief becomes the meeting place for faithful confession of belief and a request for action. Both are at work as Jesus moves into the world, bringing redemption, and grief has paved the way toward a difficult situation.

RESEARCH GRIEF

"Research grief" is what Kat Armas calls "the grief that comes when getting deep into the thick of researching difficult topics." The story Armas offers about her own journey into theology through grief is an inspiring example of the discoveries that are made possible when we allow grief space in our work as theologians. But often, this kind of research is on more than a topic, much like theology is more than just concepts. When the lives of real people become the subject matter of our discovery, we are not dealing in vague ideas or disembodied facts but hearing true and painful stories that are enough to disquiet and reconstruct us. "When beginning my research," Armas says, "I didn't know how far the rabbit trail of digging into the story of mi gente, my people, would take me. While I knew our past was painful, I was naïve and eager to take on the task of learning more about it." The story Armas discovered "involves the story of native Cubans—the Taínos—being invaded and tortured by Spain. Worse, it tells how Spain would use their imported 'Christ' to justify the greed for gold and glory." This "Christ," Armas notes, is "the one who has infiltrated much of our theology and mission efforts—the Christ who is white, elite, and of European descent." Then, this powerful question for the work of theology: "Or could there be another Christ?"[6]

---

[6]Kat Armas, *Abuelita Faith: What Women on the Margins Teach Us About Wisdom, Persistence, and Strength* (Grand Rapids, MI: Brazos, 2021), 2, 7-9.

An "outskirts of Bethany" conversation begins to take shape here. Like Martha and Mary, Armas is a theologian who has worked from a place of grief, dealing honestly with the death-dealing realities of a fallen world and allowing grief to spotlight the very place where God may be at work. The grief is amplified by the reality that the pain inflicted on her people was done in the name of the one who stepped into the Bethany sisters' own sorrow. The name of the one who brought comfort near was (ab)used to inflict pain and exact control. But her pressing question refuses to abandon the witness John offers, because surely, the Christ whom Martha confessed as Messiah is also the one who followed the pathway of pain to the heart of the matter at Mary's invitation. This Christ is the one Armas's question seeks, "the one whom many of us had been in search of, the one of los humildes, the humble."[7]

The methodological question remains: Who can show us this Christ? How might we know more of God? Can this point of pain be a place where we might know Christ more faithfully than we had before? To whom shall we tune our ears to tell us of this one who has redemptively entered into the deepest places of sorrow rather than inflict it? Who has, like Martha and Mary, ushered Jesus into those places and can teach us to do the same? They are, for Armas, those who have known him intimately. These are the "women the world overlooks, women who bear the scars of colonization." Armas issues, then, "an invitation not only to celebrate these women but to consider them genuine sources of theology."[8] In their lives and testimonies, we meet the Christ who is still being invited into places of sorrow. Lazarus stories are being told in their voices. Following the pathway into grief may open to us a more faithful vision of Christ and what he is doing in the world. Or, as the sisters of sorrow put it, "Come and see."

The fullness of Armas's discoveries awaits you in her book. My point here is that the grief stirred up by death and injustice may be a summons to a theologian to look, see, and find the humble Christ who is moving

---

[7] Armas, *Abuelita Faith*, 9.
[8] Armas, *Abuelita Faith*, 10-11.

amid grief toward the heart of sorrow. When grief is stirred by injustice, theologians are the ones who look for the movement of Christ, who is moving into those situations. Taught by Martha and Mary, we take a lamenting posture of inviting Christ to come and see and giving testimony to what this Christ does. While grief itself may not be a gentle teacher, Martha and Mary show us what we might do with the grief that is aroused by the injustices we see in our world, walking with the one who has come into the world toward the redemption he brings.

BELIEF IN CHRIST

Asking Christ to come and see the source of our grief invites another important methodological consideration that I have mentioned only in passing but calls for a more explicit treatment. I have in mind here the way Jesus does not stop at Martha's correct though somewhat vague affirmation that he is the one who "is to come into the world." John's grammar is also a bit vague; her statement could either be a present participle or passive nominative, which means she is saying that Jesus either is the one who is actively coming into the world *right now* or is one who *will* come into the world. This does not have to be a point of frustration for us, because as we have seen so often in John's writings, we are probably dealing with a both/and.

Martha's use of the term *kosmon* echoes John's use of that word to describe Jesus' cosmically large mission, especially noteworthy in Jesus' famous affirmation, "For God so loved the *kosmon* that he gave his one and only Son" (Jn 3:16). To be sure, Jesus' work is happening on a grand scale. Yet, the grandness of scale does not overlook the particularity of *this* grief, *this* death, *this* situation. The cosmic mission will not overlook Lazarus's dead body or his sisters' tears over his death. His mission, while universal in scope, also works in particulars.

We return, then, to this observation from the sisters' encounter with Jesus: while belief in the universal truths of Jesus' work and mission is not incorrect, these cannot be disconnected from the concrete particulars of the way Jesus works *here*. Put another way, if our theological method stops at the universal and conceptual truths about Christ, we may miss out on witnessing what he does in embodied and particular situations. Opening ourselves to Mary's theological instruction may allow us to locate conceptual truths in relationship to particular situations, in particular places, among particular people. Theologians trained by her may be able to say, "Look at how he is coming into the world right here!"

Doing theology in conceptual terms alone is a difficult habit to break, largely because this is the way theology tends to be presented. The sisters of Bethany, however, remind us that the confessions of Christ on a cosmic scale belong together with the particularity of situations that are causing grief in concrete places among particular people. Martha correctly says that Jesus is coming into the world; Mary invites that coming into *her* grief.

Sometimes contemporary theology departs from its methodological starting point. Some theologians, beginning from embodied points of grief, argue that their method allows for theological reflection in real situations. Other theologians, concerned that this method may tempt us create a God in the image of our preferred solution to a concrete problem, argue that the cosmic or universal approach offers a corrective to this impulse. What we see in Martha and Mary's story is that the movement of Jesus deeper and deeper into the grief-causing fallenness of the world can make these methods partners rather than adversaries. These two, after all, are sisters who are united in their grief for a brother they love.

Depending on how theology has been presented to us, we may lean toward one of these sisters more than the other. Most of the beginning theologians I encounter tend to bring an impulse toward the conceptual into their theological work. For many of them, theology is an attempt to work out cosmic concepts about things such as divine omnipotence and omniscience. They are, more often than not, deeply motivated to get their theology "right," to have the correct concepts. That is when I try to ask them about what grieves them in the world, because even if they have every concept correct, I want to be sure they can talk about what God's entrance into the world looks like, acts like, and sounds like in those places. Taking a page from Martha and Mary, I have to imagine that it looks a lot like walking with Christ to show him what has broken our hearts, allowing him to weep with us, and watching carefully to see what he does next.

PRAYER

God of comfort and peace, come and see.

Come and look upon our lives.

Come and see how we are moved to love you and offer praise.

Come and see how our hearts are grieved.

Come and see how our world suffers under our mistreatment of it
    and one another.

Come and see the beautiful things that are happening where we live,
    work, and play.

Then, show us your presence.

Show us that you are here, with us.

Teach us to work in awareness of your nearness.

Sprinkle our work with the tears your Son shed, that we might be
    moved with him,

For your glory forever and ever,

Amen.

QUESTIONS FOR DISCUSSION OR REFLECTION

1. Have you experienced God joining you in grief? How might you invite Jesus to draw near and weep with you? What possibilities do you see for how this could shape you and your approach to theology?

2. Do you identify more with Martha's grief response or Mary's? What theological avenues open in each? What could you learn from the one less familiar to you?

3. What role does lament have in your own spiritual journey and theological work? Who are the ones, as Kat Armas says, "the world overlooks," and how can you learn from their theology in lament?

CHAPTER TWELVE

Nicodemus

ON THEOLOGY AT NIGHT AND
LEADERSHIP IN THE DARK

THE MOST PUBLIC VERSE OF THE BIBLE was originally spoken in a very private conversation. The Scripture reference we see issuing forth from the bottoms of fast-food restaurant cups, the back of the long-haul truck we follow impatiently on the interstate, and some zealous football fan's hand-painted posterboard is the one that its first hearer likely never wanted anyone to overhear. He had, in fact, gone to Jesus when no one would see their meeting. The theology he hoped to do was supposed to be a secret. That is a reality we miss when we bypass the first fifteen verses of John 3 on our way to "For God so loved the world . . ." Those fifteen verses, however, tell us about the way a powerful man tried to go about doing theology with Jesus one night and the corrective word he received from his conversation partner. I am, of course, talking about Nicodemus, a Pharisee, "a member of the Jewish ruling council," and "Israel's teacher" (Jn 3:1, 10).

We are turning to Nicodemus as a theological mentor of sorts, and as we do, questions of theology's relationship to ministry, authority, and leadership begin to rise. Central to the questions we will ask of Nicodemus are those of how theology can be done virtuously, especially as it leads to the stewardship of religious authority. Ultimately, we will see that theology done in a way that is open to the bright surprise of new creation carries a transformational capacity. When theology is conducted without that kind of openness—when it is done in the dark—it often produces a calcified form of preservationism, averse to new possibilities. Adopting this kind of methodological approach and readying ourselves for the surprising light of new creation in Jesus draws us down a path of virtue, if we are willing to move our theological work out of the night and into the light of day.

Probing the shadows surrounding Nicodemus's conversation with Jesus will also allow us to explore theology's relationship with the practices of religious authority—what we sometimes call practical ministry or church leadership. Currently there is no shortage of attention being paid to leadership in religious circles, and some of that attention comes with varying amounts of theological reflection. Even more rare is attention being given to the *way* theology is done so that virtuous leadership might be the result. Nicodemus's story, however, invites us into that space. Even closer to the heart of this chapter is the question whether we approach the work of theology in such a way that whatever leadership roles we inhabit will be shaped by the truly good news of Jesus, even if it disrupts what we have previously known. As those in or preparing for positions of religious authority, we can learn theology, but does that mean we will *act* theologically when it is time to make decisions that will shape a faith community? The answer to that question, of course, is largely answered by whether we are guided by the light of new creation shining through Jesus or whether we conduct our theological business under the comfortable cover of darkness, where it can be protected against the light of truth we find in Jesus Christ.

NEW-CREATION THEOLOGY AT NIGHT

As John presents him, it is never entirely clear how committed Nicodemus was to Jesus. When we turn to him to teach us about doing the work of theology, then, we do so by taking him in his complexity. Not all mentors teach us from their successes. Not all virtue is acquired through positive examples. Often we learn from failures too. Nicodemus teaches us by what he does and by what he does not do, and we will take those together to learn about doing theology at night.

Nicodemus, like any other living person, is a complex being, stretched by competing commitments and complicated social realities. Additionally, he comes to us through John's literary lens and theological commitments, where realities such as darkness and light tend to be played off each other in dialectical ways. Rather than casting Nicodemus as a simplistic caricature, John presents him as someone operating out of a position of religious authority and leadership, who is also manifestly curious about Jesus and displays a desire for truth. He is a man living between the pressures of maintaining and preserving a religious community and the disruption Jesus threatens to bring to the community Nicodemus serves.

John's character sketch of Nicodemus calls forth empathy and challenge. On the one hand, the challenge he encounters in Jesus calls us to hope that he will rise to the occasion. On the other hand, it is hard not to be empathetic, knowing that the challenge he is facing will be disruptive to his life. Nicodemus is not a villainous figure. He is, after all, a religious leader who has given his life to doing everything the right way. It would be too easy for us to castigate him for his hesitation to cast his lot with Jesus. If we allow ourselves a moment of self-searching honesty, we may look intently at this story and find ourselves reflected back in Nicodemus's character. Who among us in a form of religious authority has not felt the strain of proclaiming a message of transformation among a people who are not keen on having their lives disrupted? Which of our religious communities and its leaders effortlessly embrace the radically new way of Jesus? There is likely a reason Jesus uses a birth metaphor with Nicodemus, the religious authority figure: giving birth is change and disruption punctuated with groaning and pain. For us to withhold empathy from Nicodemus would be to be dishonest about our own eagerness for the pangs of new birth.

Like so many religious leaders in both his time and ours, Nicodemus is an institutional preservationist, a man who has dedicated his life to maintaining his community's way of life. Maintaining that life was nothing less than what was expected of him; his own community would have forcefully reminded him that a *good* leader would not allow a new teacher with questionable credentials to upend thousands of years of tradition. Nicodemus is not an oppositional figure to Jesus; he is simply suspicious of a young firebrand rabbi who seems to have the capacity to disrupt everything Nicodemus holds dear. The question of Nicodemus's life is whether his desire for stability will allow him to embrace the holy disruption of God in flesh. Theologically, will his encounter with Jesus reorient his ministry and teaching? To use John's own literary device, will Nicodemus operate in the dark, or will he see anew by the light that has come into the world?

Without casting Nicodemus shamefully, John will not let the point escape our attention that Nicodemus comes to Jesus at night, in the dark. Does Nicodemus simply not want to be seen talking to this young, upstart teacher from Galilee, that region of unsophistication? Everything about Jesus, after all, defies the expectations of Nicodemus's closest friends and colleagues about what kind of pedigree a teacher needs to have (Jn 7:50-52). Or could it be that Nicodemus is simply a man in figurative darkness, contrasted to Jesus, who is the "true light that gives light" (Jn 1:9)?

Thankfully, John's style of writing moves beyond either-or approaches and offers a distinctive both/and. From what we see in John's Gospel, Nicodemus probably did not want to be seen in polite company with Jesus, at least not at first. He is cautious, inching closer to Jesus when the political pressure is not too heavy. At the same time, his nighttime encounter with Jesus is illuminated by what Jesus says and does. As John would have us see it, Nicodemus finds himself blinking into the challenging light, even when he tries to remain in the dark.

Like some other figures in John's Gospel, Nicodemus shows up three times, signaling a beginning, middle, and conclusion to his story. We first find him in the nighttime obscurity of John 3, an encounter with Jesus that is rhetorically riddled with the contrast between darkness and light.

Jesus slowly ratchets up "light" language throughout the encounter, finally offering this explosive conclusion:

> This is the verdict: Light has come into the world, but people loved
> darkness instead of light because their deeds were evil. Everyone who
> does evil hates the light, and will not come into the light for fear that their
> deeds will be exposed. But whoever lives by the truth comes into the light,
> so that it may be seen plainly that what they have done has been done in
> the sight of God. (Jn 3:19-21)

We have no word of how Nicodemus received this message. If we did,
perhaps it would distract from the rhetorical power of the spotlight being
turned to the reader. Do we love the darkness? If we are in a position of
religious authority, too, how comfortable are we with Jesus? Is there anything for us to fear in the light?

Nicodemus's nocturnal dialogue is also where themes of second birth
appear in the Bible. An image that has shaped countless believers since
Nicodemus, being born again—or the equally valid translation, "born
from above"—is a concept that originally confuses him. When Jesus tells
Nicodemus that he must be born again, the Pharisee wonders aloud how
a grown man can possibly reenter the womb. "Very truly I tell you," Jesus
replies, "no one can enter the kingdom of God unless they are born of
water and the Spirit. Flesh gives birth to flesh, but the Spirit gives birth
to spirit" (Jn 3:5-6). This mysterious set of metaphors that marks Nicodemus's first encounter with Jesus will take on renewed significance only
in their final meeting. From this point forward, though, every appearance
of Nicodemus comes with John's reminder: this is the man who originally approached Jesus at night.

Let us not overlook the significance, then, of Jesus speaking to a man
in religious authority about being reborn, especially because John tells
this story as part of his emphasis on new creation. The first two chapters
of John's Gospel are loaded with fascinating recalls of (re)creation motif,
from John's opening lines ("In the beginning . . ."), lifted directly from
Genesis 1, to his accounting for time by days ("The next day . . ."). Some

New Testament scholars point out that John opens his account by marking time in terms of weeks of new creation rather than simply giving a straightforward account of Jesus' ministry.[1] That is, if Genesis tells how God created, John is telling how God is re-creating through Jesus. With the light of Jesus coming into the world, a new day is dawning, and all things are being made new. The question Nicodemus faces is whether he will allow all his power, position, and authority to be reborn in new creation's morning, or whether he is too comfortable hanging out in the shadowy darkness of old creation. To ask a more methodological question, will the way Nicodemus responds to Jesus' words draw him into the virtues of the community being formed in new creation? There is something of a methodological choice given to Nicodemus: take Jesus' words so seriously that they shape his approach to religious authority or insulate himself from Jesus' challenge through a lack of exposure to the light.

The results of this conversation are ambiguous; it concludes without a declaration of rebirth from Nicodemus. Given everything John has chosen to tell us about Nicodemus—that he is a member of the ruling council, that he is coming to Jesus at night—we should not be surprised that the conversation is a bit of a struggle without a clear conclusion. That, perhaps, is where John is raising his theological question: Do you see how difficult it is for someone in a position of religious authority to be born anew? Can you feel the tension between institutional preservation and new creation? Do you see how comfortable the shadows can be when you are challenged by the light coming into the world?

I readily grant that the challenge to have all aspects of our lives reoriented to new creation is a struggle for anyone, but given John's explicit identification of Nicodemus as a person of religious authority, we should not overlook this important detail. In the dimness of night, when it is most difficult to see, this much becomes clear: Jesus has come to offer a

---

[1]See John McHugh, *John 1-4: A Critical and Exegetical Commentary* (Edinburgh: T&T Clark, 2009).

new kind of creation, all the way down. Religious power itself is being remade, because, as Jesus says to Nicodemus, "Just as Moses lifted up the snake in the wilderness, so the Son of Man must be lifted up" (Jn 3:14). It is a point that Nicodemus may not have understood until he was looking up at Jesus, lifted above the onlooking crowds as he died on a cross. Even the notion of being lifted up—elevated—requires a new birth of understanding that allows us to "see the kingdom of God" (Jn 3:3). If Nicodemus's view of religious authority was of being lifted up to a position of prestige and social status, Jesus shines a light into the shadowy night for Nicodemus, calling this powerful man and all others to a new birth into the light that will allow them to see power, authority, and leadership for what they are in the new creation Jesus brings. Again, as we consider how disruptive this recreation of authority can be, the question hovers: Are the shadows of old creation simply too comfortable for established leaders to step into the light that is coming into the world and making all things new?

TURNING OVER THEOLOGICAL TABLES

We also cannot forget that Jesus issues this challenge on the heels of one of the most disruptive acts of re-creation he committed. Rather than presenting the cleansing of the temple as one of the last events of Jesus' life, as the Synoptic Gospels (Matthew, Mark, Luke) do, John places this story in the second chapter of his Gospel, just before his encounter with Nicodemus. In that story, Jesus disrupts the entire system of temple practices that were built up around the place where God rested with creation, a kind of eighth-day-of-creation location. Since it was also the place where humans could rest in God's presence, Jesus did not let barriers to that resting stand. The temple needed to be a place where people experienced re-creation, renewed by being in God's presence, and the old-creation patterns of buying and selling had turned a place of re-creation into more of the same. The point is that new creation rarely leaves old-creation practices and patterns intact. The light coming into the world will inevitably disrupt the shadows of the old.

So when the narrative moves from the turning over temple tables to a nighttime chat with Nicodemus, the question is still in the air: Will you be the kind of religious authority who will join this new creation, or will you remain enmeshed in the old? Will you be born anew into the new creation arriving in Jesus, or will you try to negotiate Jesus into existing commitments?

Let us not shy away from it: Christian theology will turn over tables of old creation because at its heart it is a courageous movement from the shadows of old creation toward the realities breaking out when the light comes into the world. Methodologically, then, this is why theology and leadership cannot be held apart as two related but distinct fields of inquiry. Theology will always seek to shine a light on the patterns and practices that religious authority uses and ask, "Is this old creation or new creation?"

Additionally, this is also why theology cannot be approached as mere idle speculation about things that do not touch realities such as practical ministry and leadership. What Nicodemus encountered that night was not a set of ideas set apart from the fleshly world of authority and power dynamics, nor was it an encounter that would simply support the stability of his religious institution. No, Nicodemus encountered God in the flesh, coming face to face with a methodological reorientation. If he thought theology was idle speculation about things that do not affect the fleshly matters of the world, he probably was not prepared to encounter the reality that is the basis of Christian theology: *God became flesh*, and it is making everything new. If he was more interested in insulating a religious community from disruption, he probably was not prepared to encounter the reality that we cannot escape in Christian theology: *God's entrance into the world is a redemptive disruption.*

What may be more pervasive, though, is a type of methodological approach to religious authority and leadership that holds the virtues of the Christian community apart from the virtues of a set of principles and practices that fall under the title of leadership. It is the kind of strain we see in Nicodemus's life as he attempts to enact the virtues that make him a good authority figure in his religious community while seeing the truthfulness of Jesus' own way, which would most certainly disrupt his community. Nicodemus's dilemma makes it clear that the way of Jesus simply will not fit hand-in-glove into the prior commitments of a given community. Maintaining practices that make one a good leader in an old-creation community may not make one a virtuous follower of Jesus as he makes creation new. Our theological method has to adjust for this or we risk becoming the kinds of religious authorities who employ old-creation practices that are out of step with new-creation realities. The virtue of ministry leadership is found in being born again into a new creation, where the stewardship of authority is *good* when it is true to the one who is lifted up on a cross.

Methods that reduce theology to a kind of speculation about spiritual matters, holding them apart from the concrete realities of life in the real world, ignore the methodological importance of God becoming flesh. In Jesus, we theologians are confronted by a light shining on any shadowy temptation to treat theology as a prerequisite on the way to the concrete and practical matters of church leadership. God becoming flesh in Jesus is a decisive critique of any approach to ministry leadership that would find virtue in something that works even if it is out of step with the new creation. Raw effectiveness or institutional preservation is only vice if it resides in the shadows, away from the illuminating light of Jesus, resisting being born into an utterly new reality. Perhaps this is why Jesus will not let Nicodemus do this kind of theological work and challenges his leadership on this very point. "You are Israel's teacher . . . and do you not understand these things?" (Jn 3:10). Being born again—or born from above—involves a complete revolution in how religious authority is enacted. For those in religious authority, being born again gives the capacity to see the very kingdom we are called to embody. Theology is the necessary discipline of shining the light coming into the world on our habits, practices, and use of power, asking whether they reflect the light of the world. Far from being idle speculation, theology is a spiritual discipline for those in authority to evaluate whether they are enfleshing the dynamics of the new creation or have become comfortable in the shadows of old creation.

If those of us in positions of religious authority reduce Jesus to a teacher who has some interesting things to teach us about God but are not fundamentally reborn into the pattern of new creation, we are simply trying to make old wineskins hold new wine. Any form of leadership like this will most likely be consumed with patching the old skins rather than delighting in the gift of new wine (Mt 9:17; Mk 2:22). We run the risk of offering old-creation leadership strategies and tactics dressed up in clerical garb. Jesus' concern for Nicodemus, however, is that he be born anew, so that he can *see the kingdom of God*. Any use of his religious authority that operates without a vision of the kingdom of God is going to call for Nicodemus to be utterly and completely reborn.

TWILIGHT LEADERSHIP

Again, it is not entirely clear what kind of an impact Jesus' conversation has on Nicodemus. The next time we encounter him, it is in the midst of a heated debate on whether Jesus could possibly be Israel's long-awaited Messiah (Jn 7:25-52). The details of the discussion await you in a close reading of John 7, but suffice it to say here, the question of Jesus' messiahship centers on where he is from and what he is doing among the people. His teaching and works (signs, as John calls them) suggest he is God's anointed, while his hometown makes the matter of messiahship more contentious. Those familiar with the prophetic connection between the Messiah and Bethlehem cannot see how a man from Galilee—some seventy miles away from Bethlehem—could hold the hometown credentials of Israel's savior.

When the temple guards return to the Pharisees without having arrested Jesus, these men in religious authority worry that Jesus has cast some sort of spell over the guards as well, winning them over with his rhetorical charm.

"No one ever spoke the way this man does," the guards replied.

"You mean he has deceived you also?" the Pharisees retorted. "Have any of the rulers or Pharisees believed in him? No! But this mob that knows nothing of the law—there is a curse on them." (Jn 7:46-49)

There is one Pharisee, however, who raises a question. "Does our law condemn a man without first hearing him to find out what he has been doing?" Nicodemus asks (Jn 7:51).

By no stretch of the imagination is Nicodemus's question a resounding proclamation of belief in Jesus, but it can be interpreted as the shrewd question of a politically savvy man who is navigating a complex dynamic of power. At the same time, he is not joining the chorus of those ready to turn against Jesus. In short, Nicodemus is a man who stands between full belief in the new creation Jesus is bringing and the dynamics of the old creation. "Are you from Galilee, too?" his colleagues ask—a plainly rhetorical question meant as an insult, lumping Nicodemus in with the crude and uneducated rabble who come out of places like Jesus' hometown. "Look into it, and you will find that a prophet does not come out of Galilee" (Jn 7:52).

The scene ends there with Nicodemus's question lingering and his colleagues' retort stinging. Maybe Jesus is indeed the light of the world, but Nicodemus is not a man who wants that light shining on him to disrupt his social, political, and professional standing. Jesus may be the light of the world who is coming into a dark world, but Nicodemus is a man living at twilight, caught somewhere between old and new creation. He is interested in Jesus, perhaps even sympathetic, but not yet a man who has been captivated by a vision of the kingdom of God. Is this a failure of theology or a failure of leadership? In short, because these two cannot be separated, it is both at the very same time.

FROM WOMB TO TOMB

When we find Nicodemus for a third and final time, he is caring for the crucified and dead body of Jesus. Accompanying Joseph of Arimathea, who "was a disciple of Jesus, but secretly because he feared the Jewish leaders," Nicodemus secures permission from Pilate to remove Jesus' body from the cross and prepare it for burial (Jn 19:38). Together, Joseph and Nicodemus are brothers of the shadows who wait until the spotlight has faded from the darkness of the crucifixion events before entering into them.

Here now, in an arch that spans from womb to tomb, Nicodemus cares for a man in death who spoke to him about being born again. As Nicodemus's story comes to a conclusion, we are left to wonder whether he remained in the shadows or was sufficiently liberated by Jesus' message to move from darkness to light. Was Jesus' challenge to him to be born anew ever taken seriously enough that it changed the way Nicodemus used his authority? Would his brand of leadership ever come to reflect the light that was coming into the world?

We search John's writings in vain for clear answers to questions like these, but I think we have enough evidence to support a reading of this passage that sheds a hopeful light on Nicodemus. In his willingness to show up and care for Jesus' crucified body, I cannot help but wonder whether his notions of power and authority began to be reborn as he dealt with what it meant for Jesus to be lifted up. I wonder whether his first words to Jesus on that dark night, "For no one could perform the signs you are doing if God were not with him," came back to his mind as he wrapped cloth around Jesus' lifeless body. I wonder whether his notions of authority and power were undergoing a crucifixion of their own, preparing the way for the new birth of resurrection. Maybe there was enough that he had seen and heard of Jesus, maybe he was just responsive enough to the divine grace that was working in that moment, for him to catch a glimpse of way power operates in God's kingdom. In whatever future unfolded for Nicodemus, perhaps grace guided him in the use of his authority such that it was utterly and completely converted to the pattern of the new creation of the rabbi who taught with God's authority, whom he was now dressing for burial.

LEADERSHIP BORN FROM ABOVE

I will grant that my hopeful reading of Nicodemus's future is not verified in John's writing, but I think his story points to the hopeful possibility that opens to each of us. The gift in his story is an opportunity to use whatever authority we have been granted to operate entirely out of a vision of God's kingdom. It is an opportunity to leave behind the shadows of old-creation power dynamics and be born anew into a Christlike stewardship of authority. This gift, however, is also a call for rigorous theological reflection. Leadership training often reminds us that we have to have a vision of where we are going. Theology is the discipline that helps us know whether the vision we have is faithful to God. It enlivens our vision with the light that has come into the world through Jesus Christ. It calls us to examine our practices and ask whether they are reflecting the light of Jesus Christ. Theology gives us the vital capacity to reflect on what we have done and what we are doing in ministry leadership, and to expose our actions to the light of Christ.

Doing theology in the dark, however, is like refusing to allow our leadership decisions to be brought to the light. Nicodemus's encounter with Jesus reminds us that those in positions of religious authority may be tempted to come to Jesus while giving ourselves the cover of darkness, stepping toward Jesus to gain a few interesting ideas but shirking the challenge to allow our authority to be completely reborn according to a vision of the kingdom of God. Authorities who deal with the light of the world only at night stand little chance of being born from above.

Drawing from a story told by Theophane, a monk living in Colorado, Ruth Haley Barton finds insight for the life of those who are called to leadership. As the story goes, Theophane saw another monk working alone in a vegetable garden one day. After approaching him and asking him what his dream was, the other monk replied that he wanted to be a monk. Confused, Theophane pointed out that this garden-working man was already a monk. It was then that the man pulled back his robe to reveal the revolver that he had carried for all twenty-five years of his cloistered life. "I've been hurt a lot," the armed monk confessed, "and I've hurt a lot of others. I don't think I would be comfortable without this gun." After pointing out that having the gun seemed to be making him uncomfortable, Theophane asked whether his companion would give him the gun. Through tears, the monk released his weapon as the two embraced.[2]

---

[2]Ruth Haley Barton, *Strengthening the Soul of Your Leadership: Seeking God in the Crucible of Ministry* (Downers Grove, IL: InterVarsity Press, 2018), 55-56.

Barton goes on to ask her readers to reflect on whether they carry a proverbial gun. What is it that we might hold on to, to refuse to release, a years-long practice that we hide under the garments of our calling but do not allow to be converted? Barton has in mind protective patterns of self-preservation, but we can also apply this to patterns and practices of leadership that seem as out of place to the way of Jesus as a revolver does strapped to the waist of a monk. When we are tempted to use tactics because they have worked in the past or to employ the power of our authority in ways that remain unconverted, it is likely that we are doing theology in the dark.

The gift to us in the work of theology is its capacity to expose unconverted places, habits, commitments, and practices. It is the crucial reflection on the practical work of ministry that not only offers us a vision of God's kingdom but also measures whether our work is consistent with the dynamics of that kingdom.

Of course, a good deal of what passes for Christian ministry is done in theological darkness. For a host of reasons ranging from remaining relevant to making sure the message of the gospel remains accessible, habits, practices, and even language can be vaguely associated with Jesus but not converted to his kingdom. While they may be effective at producing results, the theological question is what kind of kingdom these results are serving. Or the methodological question is, What approach to theology have you taken that assumes it can be held apart from the worked realities of Christian ministry?

WHY THEOLOGY DOES NOT APPLY TO MINISTRY

The underlying methodological question here has to do with whether and how theology can be applied to things such as the practice of ministry and religious leadership. Nicodemus's original approach began with a similar question. Approaching Jesus as a teacher who might offer some insights he could apply to life, Nicodemus ends up being redemptively surprised by a profound reality: theology does not *apply* to ministry. The practice of ministry *is* theology in flesh. It is the shape of theology lived out. The question is, Does this set of practices look at all like the new creation of Jesus Christ? Does it only make sense in light of Jesus, crucified and resurrected?

A pervasive bit of methodological malpractice relegates theology to a theoretical and speculative enterprise, while matters of ministry are worked out "in the real world" by practitioners. In this approach, we can either apply theology or not, because theology and ministry are somehow fundamentally disconnected. Alister McGrath puts a fine point on this divide when he asks, "Why waste time teaching future Christian leaders about theology when they could instead feast on the latest theories of church growth, congregational management and counseling skills?"[3]

I join my voice to McGrath's assessment of the methodological assumptions that give us a question like that: "I can't help but feeling that they've not been properly thought through." Or, at least, a question like this one points to the fact that theology done in such a way that it is hard to relate to ministry points to unexamined methodological problems. "Nobody wants to devote time and resources to doing something that is pointless," McGrath concedes. "But what if theology sustains the vision that lies at the heart of Christian faith? What if theology has a unique and necessary role to play in keeping this vision alive and thus energizing and sustaining the life, worship and outreach of the Church?"[4] We could ask the question with Nicodemus in mind: What happens when religious authority operates without a clear vision of the kingdom of God? What does religious authority look like when it is formed at night, suspicious of or resistant to the light of the world?

Theology is the vital work of being captivated by a vision of what God is doing and putting into words that vision for the sake of faithful life, mission, and worship. It may begin at night, but it is always searching for morning, informed by the light that has come into the world. It is the

---

[3]Alistair McGrath, *What's the Point of Theology? Wisdom, Wellbeing, and Wonder* (Grand Rapids, MI: Zondervan Academic, 2022), 7.
[4]McGrath, *What's the Point of Theology?*, 7.

ongoing reflective work of seeing God's activity and asking, "How can we live most faithfully to that reality?" Theology carries the necessary task of pointing to the redemptive work of God, asking how the church might be most vitally engaged in it, and evaluating whether our words and work are faithful. In other words, theology is always attempting to draw us into the light.

Theology, then, is not theoretical thought-work done apart from practical ministry. Theology asks whether our practices are a faithful response to the light that is coming into the world. It gives us the capacity to look at what we are doing, or being asked to do, and evaluate whether those actions are faithful. Theology gives practice a vitally necessary vision of where it needs to go. Or, to return to McGrath's words, "A theologian is someone who cultivates the habit of discernment: seeing things rightly, properly and fully."[5] As we have learned from Nicodemus, it is hard to see in the dark. You may have lots of authority and power, but when you are trying to operate at night, hesitating on whether you can be all in on new creation, all of that authority will not take you very far in the dynamics of God's kingdom.

Reflecting on the relationship of the practice of ministry to theology, Stanley Hauerwas relates a story, perhaps apocryphal, about a longtime Methodist pastor who was listening to a debate unfold about a professor who was teaching at a nearby Methodist seminary. At issue was the matter of original sin and whether this particular professor was teaching a version of the doctrine that was out of step with the denominational position. After listening to the conversation, the minister's increasing frustration got the best of him. "Finally, unable to listen to one more argument for or against original sin, he rose declaring that he had had it with all this theological hair-splitting. After all, he said, little depends on theological opinions because, as they all know, most of theology is bunk. What they must do, he argued, is forget theology and preach Christ and him crucified."[6]

---

[5]McGrath, *What's the Point of Theology?*, 15.
[6]Stanley Hauerwas, *The Work of Theology* (Grand Rapids, MI: Eerdmans, 2015), 104.

The irony, of course, is that in his attempt to dismiss the practicality of theology, the minister was making a profound claim about the vital role of theology in ministry. Woven into the logic of his claim is a centering of the crucified and risen Christ, pointing to a crucial theological task: evaluating whether what we are doing makes any sense at all in light of Jesus. That is, if the actions of the church or leader only make sense in the light of Jesus, theology's work is probably holding true. If, however, there are tactics, approaches, or strategies in use that make sense according to some other logic but seem out of step with Christ's way, theology's task is just as vital: point out where our practice is out of step with the light of the world. If our approach to theology is such that we can remain in the shadows, at arm's length from the light of the world, something is methodologically amiss. The good news, however, is this: the light has come into the world, and the darkness has not overcome it.

PRAYER

God of light, shine on us that we may see.
God of life, grant that we may be born anew.
For the sake of your Son, Jesus Christ, fill us with your Holy Spirit,
That we may be made in his likeness for your glory.
The creation you made and love groans as if in childbirth.
Allow us by your grace to attend carefully to this new birth.
Give us eyes to see the new creation being born within the old,
And the wisdom to discern the practices that align most faithfully
     with your coming into the world.
Grant us, we ask, hearts that long for your new creation.
Move us gently away from our commitments and comforts that hold us
     back from joining fully into the way you are making all things new.
Amen.

QUESTIONS FOR DISCUSSION OR REFLECTION

1. How can you identify theology done in the dark, resistant to the light of new creation? Do you see this happening anywhere right now, whether in you or in your community?

2. In what ways can you relate to Nicodemus or to a specific point in his journey? Are you now holding on to any old patterns and practices of leadership that are out of place in the light of new creation?

3. Why is it often so difficult to move beyond the preservation instincts of a good leader in old-creation communities in order to embrace Jesus' disruptive new creation? What virtues and/or fruit of the Spirit are needed for a person to live and lead in this way of Jesus?

Conclusion

I AM STANDING ON THE BROAD BED of dark green grass we have come to simply call "the meadow," flanked on one side by a clear, lazy creek on steady course to empty itself into a waiting mountain pond as the sun is sinking behind the pines. Children are running the expanse of the campground in energetic packs, excitedly seeking out nighttime adventures, newly freed from the bonds of their parents asking them to sit still during an open-air worship service that has just concluded at our annual family camp.

"Are you sure you don't want to come with us?" a friend asks. I am not sure. Something inside me wants to set out with them on this hurriedly planned excursion to hike all night in time to arrive at an overlook in nearby Yosemite National Park, simply to watch the sunrise. I am caught between an imagined future where I am among this brazen band of adventurers, seated on the elevated granite as the black sky begins to glow with purples and reds over the picturesque valley, and a version of the immediate future in which I am tucked warmly into my cabin for a night of sleep, awakening well-rested.

"It sounds incredible," I hear myself say in response. "I'd better not, though." I am not sure I believe my own words. My friends disappear into the night and I retire to my cabin, wondering whether I have made the right decision.

I often wonder what would have happened had I accepted that invitation. I caught up with my friends the next morning as they returned from their adventure. Passionate descriptions of their excursion poured out of them like water breaching a dam. They told me about the physical dangers they faced while traversing steep terrain in the dark. They held forth about the unparalleled sight of morning light spilling over ancient rock formations into the valley below. Apparently, songs of praise to God spontaneously broke out among them, the only response appropriate to the glory of the moment.

I like to tell this story when I need a way to illustrate the way doctrine has formed in the church's long history. Doctrine can be a lot like a group of people searching for the best words they can find to describe to others what they have encountered. When you have had an encounter that cannot be contained in words but you just cannot help but talk about it, you still find the best words you can to describe the reality, even if you need to make a few up along the way (such as *homoousios* and *hypostasis*). "We encountered God in the flesh!" I can hear them say. "It's astoundingly good and true and beautiful. Let me tell you about it!" And the dam breaks.

Christian theology is, of course, more than watching a sunrise. As beautiful as they are, mountaintop experiences are still finite—they are fleeting and limited. Part of theology's work is to describe a God who is infinite, boundless goodness. So, my hope is that you will accept an invitation to the theological life. Undoubtedly, we could easily opt for a more comfortable, less adventurous pathway, but I often wonder how I would have been shaped by accepting the invitation that came to me that night on the meadow.

Gladly, Scripture is filled with the stories of helpful guides. Jeremiah, Isaiah, Miriam, Jacob, Martha, and those in their company offer us the example of their lives as they respond to God. They are not alone, of course, and I hope that our interactions with them will illuminate others in Scripture's story who might help develop us into people who do the work of theology with joy, excellence, and virtue. The work of theology will not look identical for all of us on the journey, and drawing from the deep well of Scripture will sustain us by developing further virtues.

Maybe someday that group will make the hike through the night again. If they invite me, I like to think I would take them up on the offer, and that the trip would offer not only something I could not encounter from the comfort of my cabin but also something of the virtues of exploration that I could learn from those who have done this kind of thing before. I like to think that I would watch how they navigated the trails and responded to the experience as it was unfolding. With hope, I would pick up on how they made the journey well and came to know the deep joy they found in summiting a mountain and being stunned to silence—only to use their remaining energy to tell others what they have seen and invite them on the journey. Good guides are a gift. The invitation stands open.

Glossary

allegorical method	An approach to reading Scripture in which the meaning of the text is found primarily in its spiritual meaning, which may be "hidden" underneath the plain meaning of the text. This method was used widely during the patristic era.
apophatic theology	This theological method involves speaking about who God is based on who we know God is not. For example, since we know God is not evil, we might speak of God as good. It is also known as negative theology.
Asian theology	A form of contextual theology seeking to explore the Bible and theology through the lens of those living on the continent of Asia. This approach tends to be narrative and holistic in nature.
biblical theology	Seeking to allow the Bible to speak for itself, biblical theology attempts to speak theologically unaided by sources outside of the biblical canon. It is wary of "harmonizing" the Bible, especially by use of outside categories or agendas.
canonical criticism	Taking the biblical canon as a whole, this method does theology asking what the books of the Old Testament and New Testament have to say together. Rather than looking to

	individual texts, it attempts to let Scripture speak as a whole.
Christocentrism	Seen especially in the work of Karl Barth and Dietrich Bonhoeffer, this method works from Christ as the central reality and theme of theology. In Bonhoeffer's iteration, Christ mediates all of life to the disciple, thus, he is the *mitte* (middle, center) of all of life.
Christology	The study of the person and work of Jesus Christ.
contemporary theology	Generally, a term referring to the various theologies and methodologies currently in use and those developed within the last century.
demythologizing	A method developed by Rudolf Bultmann in the twentieth century, this approach attempts to modernize the reading of Scripture by replacing ancient "myths" found in the text with ideas more at home in a scientific society. Miracles, demons, and the like are largely excluded in demythologization.
dialectical theology	In dialectical theology as a method, theological significance is located in the relationship between two paradoxical or opposing realities. For example, dialectical theology will give attention to relationships such as God/humanity, Creator/creation, and so on.
dictation theory	The theory of inspiration in which the Spirit of God gave the biblical writers the precise words to write. Thus, the text should be read without attention given to the author's time and cultural setting.
doctrine	Most simply, a doctrine is a teaching of a church or religious community. It is often an attempt

	to explain or describe theological realities for the sake of belief and practice.
dogmatics	Often interpreted as carrying the weight of official doctrine, dogmatics refers to a doctrinal teaching.
ecclesiology	The study of the church's being and mission.
epistemology	The study of knowledge, especially how one comes to know and the sources of this knowledge.
eschatology	A term used to name the theological examination of the last things, especially what occurs with creation.
experience	Often considered as a source of theological reflection, referring to a human being's set of lived realities.
feminist theology	As a method, feminist theology attempts to offer theological reflection that gives attention to the experience of women. Feminist theology will often highlight a female perspective, whether that be in female biblical characters or in the lives of historic and contemporary women.
foundationalism	An approach to theology that attempts to begin from a singular starting point. "God is love" is one example of a foundational statement from which a theological system may be established.
Heilsgeschichte	The German word for "salvation history." Methodologically, this approach seeks to work theologically from seeing human history as the setting in which God's salvation is playing out.
Hermeneutics	This is the study of how we interpret texts, especially the Bible, asking the question: How

	might we most faithfully go about understanding the meaning of this text? What should our method of interpretation be?
historical criticism	An approach to biblical interpretation in which the historical situation is privileged, as opposed to a divine meaning. Often, this approach seeks the meaning "under" or "behind" the text, rather than locating the meaning in the text itself.
liberation theology	Born in Latin American contexts through the work of Gustavo Gutierrez and others, this method emphasizes God's liberating work, particularly in the exodus. It favors liberating action over contemplation, and now functions as an umbrella term for various forms of liberation theology, including African-American/ Black liberation theology, feminist theology, Asian theology, and more.
liminal	An "in-between" state or space. Often, this refers to the meaning that emerges from a space between two other spaces. In theology, it can also refer to the time between one's death and resurrection.
method	Most simply, the way one goes about their theological work. This can refer to their philosophical beginning points and commitments, or the sources one chooses and why. Methodological considerations usually revolve around questions of what theology is, what sources should be incorporated into theology, and how theology ought to function as a discipline.
natural theology	An approach to theology in which knowledge of God can be derived from the natural

creation. A person may derive knowledge of the Creator, for example, by observing a piece of the creation.

Pneumatology
The study of the person and work of the Holy Spirit.

post-liberal theology
Established in the twentieth century in the work of Hans Frei, George Lindbeck, and others, this approach to theology tends to lean on the established norms, stories, and traditions of particular communities. It is a reaction against liberal theology, and as such, embeds theological reflection in communal stories and practices.

process theology
A method based on the philosophy of twentieth century philosopher Alfred North Whitehead. Process theology tends to emphasize reality as being "in process," such that God and creation exist in relationship to one another.

realized eschatology
A method of studying eschatology by placing emphasis on the aspects of the new creation that God has already brought into reality, or "realized."

reason
In theological method, reason can be employed as a means of evaluating a theological claim, especially through the application of logic. It is often understood to be a human capacity, distinguishing it from revelation.

revelation
Generally, revelation is knowledge that comes from a source outside or beyond human capacity. In some theological methods, such as neo-orthodoxy, it is emphasized for its capacity to critique and correct theological ideals that

have been distorted by human commitments and agendas. In theology, it is often distinguished from reason, or the human capacity to gain knowledge.

scholasticism
A term used to refer to theology done in Europe in the Middle Ages, it often specifically refers to the work done by Thomas Aquinas. Methodologically, scholasticism tends to depend on philosophy, especially the work of Plato and Aristotle, to expand upon or clarify Christian doctrine.

Sola Scriptura
This Latin phrase meaning "by Scripture alone," speaks to the theological conviction coming out of the Reformation that Scripture is the sole source of authority for the Christian in faith and practice.

special revelation
A form of revelation that typically refers to the unique and most direct forms of revelation, namely the person of Jesus Christ, his place in Israel's history, and the Scriptures that testify to him.

systematic theology
An approach to theology in which emphasis is placed on harmonizing the various doctrines in a logically connected system. Though not all systematic theologies make the same claims about God and God's activities in the world, they are largely all concerned with describing the teachings of the Christian faith in coherent ways, such that one doctrine does not contradict another.

tradition
Methodologically, tradition is often used to evaluate the viability of certain theological claims. Tradition often refers to the knowledge

	that was passed to us from the apostles, especially in the form of Scripture and the Creeds.
verbal inspiration	The theory that the Spirit of God inspired the biblical writers in a way that guided the writers, but did not prescribe the exact words used. Thus, elements of the author's time and culture become aspects of the text.
womanist theology	An approach to theology that gives specific attention to the experience of Black women.

General Index

Scripture Index